LETTERS ON PSALMODY:

A REVIEW OF THE

LEADING ARGUMENTS FOR THE EXCLUSIVE USE

OF THE

BOOK OF PSALMS.

BY

WILLIAM ANNAN,

AUTHOR OF "DIFFICULTIES OF ARMINIAN METHODISM," "GOTTESCHALC'S LETTERS TO PROF. YOUNG," ETC.

"And they (in heaven) sung a new song, saying with a loud voice, WORTHY IS THE LAMB THAT WAS SLAIN." Rev. 5: 9–12.

PHILADELPHIA:
WILLIAM S. & ALFRED MARTIEN,
No. 606 CHESTNUT STREET.
1859.

STEREOTYPED BY W. S. HAVEN, PITTSBURGH, PA.

CONTENTS.

LETTER I.

LETTER II.

LETTER III.

LETTER IV.

LETTER IX.

LETTER X.

LETTER XI.

LETTER XII.

LETTER XIII.

LETTER XIV.

APPENDIX.

PREFACE.

Several years ago it was suggested to the author, by one of our most energetic and useful ministers, an honored pastor in the Presbyterian church, to undertake "the preparation of a small popular work on Psalmody." This request was enforced by the kindest considerations of a personal nature, and the brother was pleased to add: "we need a popular treatise * * * to meet the public demand on this subject." Many circumstances conspired to forbid compliance with this suggestion until a recent period. The result is now with great diffidence submitted to the Christian public.

The providential circumstances which have seemed to demand some further *defense* of the cherished usages of the Presbyterian church in relation to the public and private singing of the praises of God, are fully stated in the progress of this discussion, and especially in the Introductory Letter. If our system of Psalmody be such as is described in the quotations made from the writings of the brethren whom we oppose, *then the sooner it is abandoned the better;* since it must be, as they are pleased to allege, "a *corruption* of Divine worship" of a very offensive and dangerous sort. But if, on the other hand, it is clearly demonstrable that these brethren have misapprehended, and therefore, greatly misrepresented the views and usages of our church; if, moreover, their confident and peculiar claims to the exclusive use of an "inspired Psalmody" can be shown to be altogether without foundation; a superstructure without a basis either in the Holy Scriptures, Church History or fact; then it becomes an obvious duty to present the evidence which clearly establishes these positions. This has been attempted in the following Letters.

We disclaim at the outset, the slightest intentional disrespect toward the Psalmody in use among these brethren, by the employment in this work of the phraseology, "Rouse's versification," "Rouse's paraphrase," &c. We are told, indeed, "that to call the Divine songs *in this version*, 'Rouse's Psalms,' is to evidence gross ignorance or something worse."* Yet Neal, the distinguished historian of the Puritans, employs the phrase, "Rouse's Psalms in metre."† And what is much more to the point, the General Assembly of the Church of Scotland—1644-1649—in their formal acts authorizing that versification, employ not less than *twenty times* the phrase "Rouse's paraphrase of the Psalms," and similar terms. In such excellent company, we cannot be justly chargeable with intentional contempt of the Psalmody of these brethren, though we use the expressions referred to. We admit that the Scottish General Assembly revised and amended Rouse's work; but probably did not alter it to as great an extent as Dr. Watts' "paraphrase" has been changed from the original of Dr. W. Yet this does not prevent these brethren from using the epithet "Watts' Psalms," though in strictness of speech they are not so.

In the numerous quotations in the following Letters from leading works of these brethren, such as "M'Master's Apology," "Pressly on Psalmody," "Testimony of the United Presbyterian Church," &c. it has been the constant aim of the author to let them speak for themselves; as it was his earnest wish to meet their arguments in their own chosen forms. In reference, however, to a number of remarkable extracts from "The United Presbyterian," Cincinnati, it is only an act of justice to say that the editors of that paper, viz. the late Dr. Claybaugh, and Rev. James Prestley, now of Pittsburgh, were not personally responsible. The extracts referred to, are chiefly from communications over the signature of "Pastor." How far the editors were prepared to indorse the views of "Pastor," we can only conjecture; though one or more editions of his articles in pamphlet form were printed for wider circulation.

The zeal of these brethren for their favorite Psalmody does not seem to flag. Since the organization of "the United Presby-

* Pressly on Psalmody, p. 178.

† History of the Puritans, vol. 2, p. 42. Francis Rouse was a lay member of the Westminster Assembly of Divines, in 1643.

terian church," about twelve months ago, they have issued a "Testimony" against the supposed errors of other denominations, not overlooking this subject. Over 20,000 copies of "the Testimony," if we are rightly informed, have already been put in circulation. In addition, a new work directed more especially against "the corruption" of singing hymns, has within a few months been published in Philadelphia, and circulated in the West. A venerable Professor, too, has been employing the pulpit at home and abroad, in the same cause, warning the people against the great inconsistency, and, if his theory be the true one, the *imminent peril* of those who mingle in devotional meetings which employ other than "the inspired Psalmody." To obviate in some measure these varied efforts to perpetuate what the author is constrained to view as mischievous error, and to contribute his mite to remove a needless source of division in the Church of Christ, is the object of this treatise.

Having submitted his manuscript to several honored brethren in the ministry, the author has great pleasure in presenting to the public the appended testimonials:

Rev. W. Annan:

Dear Brother:—The undersigned have perused with great pleasure, the Letters on Psalmody you were pleased to put in their hands, and are happy to express their approbation of them. The principal arguments of those who contend for the exclusive use of "Rouse's version of the Psalms" in the worship of God, are fairly stated and completely refuted; and whilst you discuss your theme with candor and vigor, we are happy to observe it is in an eminently Christian temper.

Although there are already several excellent treatises on this subject, your letters fill a gap in this controversy, as you appear to us to meet the arguments of those from whom we differ at a number of points which others have not touched.

A clear, brief and courteous discussion of this whole subject, such as you have here furnished, is, in our judgment, much needed at this time; and the publication of what you have written, we are persuaded, through the Divine blessing, would do much to correct erroneous opinions, and to increase the attachment of our people to a Psalmody which embraces the New Testament as well as the Old, and speaks of Calvary as well as of Zion.

We hope you will consent to give these Letters to the public, and trust they may have an extensive circulation, and that their publication may result in the edification of God's people and the glory of his name.

Yours, fraternally,

W. D. HOWARD,
W. M. PAXTON.

ALLEGHENY CITY, March 11th, 1859.

REV. W. ANNAN:

Dear Brother:—Having with much pleasure perused your "Letters on Psalmody," I very cordially concur in the expressions of the foregoing letter from the pastors of the First and Second churches of this city.

Respectfully, yours,

A. O. PATTERSON.

PITTSBURGH, May 13th, 1859.

The writer does not deem it necessary to occupy his pages with further testimonials. He will only add, that having read some of the most important parts of his work to the learned and honored Professor of Theology in the Western Seminary, Dr. PLUMER after "examining *the plan* of the whole discusssion," addressed to the author a very kind note, from which the following is an extract:

"The result is, that I have no doubt your work is such as is called for by the exigency of our times. I therefore cordially commend it to the perusal of 'Zion's friends and mine.' I have great confidence that the Rev. Dr. Howard, Rev. Wm. M. Paxton and Rev. Dr. Patterson, have given a fair and just view of the whole work." It may be proper to add, that Dr. Plumer having at that time only partially recovered from a long and painful illness, and his official duties in the Seminary having greatly accumulated, was unable, though *desirous*, to peruse the whole discussion.

In concluding this Preface, we may be permitted to add a few words for the prayerful consideration of the brethren who dissent from our views. Agreeing as we do in the great fundamentals of the Calvinistic faith and of Christian morals, let us inquire seriously and earnestly, whether we are not also substantially ONE in the ordinance of praise. In *theory* we differ, but in *practice* the disagreement ceases to be a matter of principle. Just as every pious Arminian when on his knees, becomes a Calvinist; so do these brethren habitually forsake the *exclusive theory* and practice in part on the principle which we adopt. So at least it seems to us. We appeal to the ensuing argument to prove that they worship God to a large extent, in the use of "human composition."

As to the injurious and even fatal consequences flowing from these needless divisions, especially in the sparse settlements of our country, they are only too obvious and deplorable. How often does it occur, that two church edifices must be built in a neighborhood where not *one* can be half filled with worshipers — two ministers must labor where not *one* can be half supported, &c. Hence for more than half the year *silent Sabbaths* — while heresy and delusion of every shade are spreading their soul-destroying influences into every nook and corner of the land. Thus in numerous instances are the professed friends of the Lord Jesus found working into the hands of the great adversary of souls.

With these remarks we commend the work to the blessing of "the Father of lights and of wisdom, from whom cometh down every good and perfect gift," with the earnest prayer that it may be made the humble instrument of promoting the union of Christians and the salvation of souls.

PITTSBURGH, May, 1859.

LETTER I.

INTRODUCTORY REMARKS — ORIGIN OF THE WORK—EXTRACT FROM A LETTER FROM AN INQUIRING FRIEND — UNHAPPY EXAGGERATION OF OUR VIEWS — OUR USAGES MISREPRESENTED — NOTICE OF DRS. WATTS AND LATTA — DR. PRESSLY FORMERLY ON THE PRESBYTERIAN PLATFORM — HIS VIEWS OF "TRADITIONS OF THE ELDERS" — PLAN OF THE DISCUSSION PURSUED IN THIS TREATISE.

MY DEAR SIR:—I received in due season your very acceptable communication, and return you my grateful acknowledgments for the many kind expressions it contains. It is true, as you intimate, that under the force of circumstances beyond my control, my attention has been at different times directed to the subject which has occasioned your letter. Nor do I consider myself at liberty to disregard suggestions which have had an origin such as that to which you refer. That the Christian public, before which these Letters will probably appear, may understand these allusions, I take the liberty of making some extracts from your letter, as follows :

"During a recent visit among distant relatives, there was placed in my hands, and earnestly recommended to my perusal, a copy of a work entitled 'An Apology for the Book of Psalms.' In turning over its pages I confess the impressions made upon my mind were anything but pleasant, and I must add, by no means favorable to the Presbyterian church.

"I was born of parents, who, as you are aware, were of the old Scottish stock, and my excellent father was for many years a minister of the Associate Reformed church. I had been accustomed from early youth, to what is called 'the old Psalmody,' both in public and private worship, and have many of its stanzas still familiar to my memory. But when, as I grew up, I experienced those deep religious impressions, which, as I trust, were the evidence of the 'effectual call' of God's Spirit, and when I united with a church under the care of the General Assembly, it was certainly without the remotest suspicion that I thereby renounced, even by implication, any of 'the great and precious' principles of Divine truth, in which I had been so carefully trained by my honored parents.

"Judge then of my painful surprise, when there was handed to me a work whose very title indicates that a most precious portion of God's sacred word had been seriously assailed and its Divine inspiration bitterly impugned by the very branch of the church with which I had cast in my lot. That for this reason, the author referred to had felt it to be incumbent upon him to enter the controversial arena in defense of the book of Psalms—very much as some of the early fathers wrote 'apologies' for Christianity, which were designed to obviate and rebuke the malignant assaults of Jews and Pagans against the rising power and influence of the religion of Christ!

"On looking through the volume, I found the General Assembly of our church charged with 'the *entire rejection* of the inspired book of Psalms from the church's Psalmody, and the substitution of others of *human device* in their place'—and several authors belonging to the Presbyterian body are professedly quoted as employing 'arguments most popular and frequently used' * * 'representing those Divine compositions (the Psalms of David) as *Christless*,' and of course, '*almost*, if not *altogether* contrary to the spirit of the Gospel,' pp. 51, 67, 69. Again, the author charges 'that most numerous and influential body of professors (the Presbyterian church) with abandoning the songs of inspiration and practically declaring them unfit for Christian lips,' p. 85. And he solemnly testifies 'against those who have entered into these views.'

"Such, Rev. Sir, are a few specimens of the spirit and substance of the book — imposing, as the author intimates, *a necessity* upon him to step forward to shield a most precious part of revealed truth from the 'bitter libels' and the 'unhallowed suggestions uttered against it.' And in endeavoring to trace these evils to their source, he without hesitation ascribes them 'to the principles of *Infidelity* which had extended to every department both of Church and State.'*

"Having only recently commenced my preparatory studies for the ministry, and never been placed in circumstances where it became necessary to examine with much care the Psalmody question, you, Rev. Sir, can readily conceive with what impressions I perused such paragraphs as the foregoing. Could it be possible there was the slightest foundation for allegations such as these? Certainly from some considerable acquaintance with the ministry and membership of the Presbyterian church, I had never conceived the smallest suspicion of such a state of feeling toward the productions of 'the sweet Psalmist of Israel;' but on the contrary had always met with expressions of the most profound *veneration* and *esteem* for that delightful manual of devotion, especially as a component part of the 'holy oracles.' And in regard to my own experience, from the earliest dawn of religion in my soul, I had been in the habit of resorting to that precious book, the Psalms, as a most abundant fountain of light, consolation and refreshment for all classes of pilgrims to the heavenly land. Moreover, this I knew to be a common experience in the Presbyterian church. Still, as these grave charges were made by men venerable for years and respected for their talents, the only alternative left me was to express my conviction of an *utter mistake* as to matter of fact, or to remain entirely silent in regard to statements which I was not prepared to refute."

These paragraphs sufficiently define the circumstances which produced the letter of my correspondent. His experience is by no means singular. In the same letter

* The latest edition was published in 1852.

he mentions the case of a Presbyterian lady, who had never made herself acquainted with the merits of the Psalmody question—who, having placed in her hands a copy of the same work ("Apology, &c.") was so impressed with its confident assertions, that she declared to her pastor her full determination never again to employ the Psalmody of the Presbyterian church.*

In like manner those whose circumstances have brought them in contact for any considerable length of time with the books, periodicals, &c. of these brethren, must have often been grieved and indignant at the tone of rash, unbrotherly assertion which frequently appears in connection with this subject. Charges of "Infidel flouts"—"*impious rejection* of the Psalms which God has given"—"*infamous* conduct in *setting aside* the God-made hymn book and adopting man-made hymn books"—"disregard of Divine authority, want of reverence for the Scriptures, and low views in relation to their inspiration"—"speaking reproachfully of the book of Psalms"—"daring presumption"—"daring profanity"—"sentiments derogatory to the Spirit of inspiration"—"crime verging on the sin against the Holy Ghost." These are copied from the most respectable sources, from the writings of men of years and standing in their own denominations; and several of them from the official "TESTIMONY" recently issued by the Associate and Associate Reformed, now known as "the United Presbyterian body!"

In regard to the practical working of our Psalmody, the following *extraordinary* statement was published in two of their leading magazines,† issued in Philadelphia, viz:

"The Puritan churches in Old and New England, and also the two General Assemblies (Old and New School) in the States, are beacons *too alarming* to be disregarded. In these churches they have renounced the Bible Psalms,

* She soon after joined the Seceders.

† Christian Instructor and Evangelical Repository, for June, 1854; edited by Drs. Dales and Cooper.

and adopted Watts' and other collections. The experience of these churches is, that when human hymns were introduced they were not generally sung by the congregation: that was *left with the leader and a few others.* Then a choir was needed to keep up the volume of sound considered respectable. This, ere long, got stale, and became uninteresting. They then introduced organs and all sorts of 'dead instruments giving sound;' this more and *more killed congregational singing.* Then they multiplied hymn books without end: (a gentleman in New York lately carried four hymn books to church, and only one out of the four hymns sung was in the four books.) The result is, *that nobody out of the choir now sings, and the churches are literally without praise*—the most interesting and celestial exercise of the church on earth, perhaps in heaven."

It is not necessary to extend these quotations. Sufficient has been given to indicate the tone and spirit with which this controversy is conducted by the more *sober* and *mature* minds among these brethren. Neither do we propose at present to say a word to *expose* these singular allegations. Most of them will come in review as we proceed in the discussion. Charity demands that we presume their authors *thought "they were speaking the truth in love!"* Even *good men*, as all experience testifies, when they become heated by controversy, may be deceived, and unintentionally deceive others. David himself admits that he spoke "in haste," when he uttered a certain sweeping condemnation.

To revert for a moment to the particular *work* referred to by our correspondent—the extracts professedly given from the treatises of the late Dr. James Latta and two or three others, we have not the means of testing by a reference to the books themselves. They are out of print. Nor have we ever seen Dr. Latta's work, except a single copy some years since, in the private library of Rev. Dr. M'Gill, who had been a Seceder clergyman! That Dr. L. never designed to utter most of the sentiments attributed to him, is plain to my mind from several considerations: they are in direct contradiction to the whole tenor of his honored and useful life. So that it is much easier to believe that the author of the "Apology" in the heat of contest has mistaken his meaning, than to conceive that Dr. L. ever meant to express some of the sentiments ascribed to him; and the same thing is true of the others. If, however, any *opinions* on Psalmody have been uttered by any member or minister of the Presbyterian body, such as some of those imputed to Dr. L. and others, *let them be condemned!* Every sound Presbyterian will add his *amen* to the sentence. Let the volumes be produced and the quotations verified—*then* we will join these brethren in their earnest repudiation of them.

As to the professed quotations from Dr. Watts, his case will receive, as it deserves, a more particular notice. He was the honored instrument, in the hand of Providence, in arranging and versifying the Psalms and Hymns as they are generally used in our churches; and he has met with no ordinary share of abuse and misrepresentation. Suffice it to say for the present, that as our Psalmody has been repeatedly revised with great care, by large and respectable committees of the General Assembly, the system now bears the official sanction of that body. The views of Psalmody uttered by Dr. W. in his "Essay" and "Prefaces," have never been indorsed by our Assembly. They may be true or false—*they are not ours.* So also with the *reasons* Dr. W. assigns for certain changes introduced into parts of the Psalms. The General Assembly have sanctioned and adopted many of those alterations, with their own amendments—but *not one* of the published *reasons* of Dr. Watts.* We wish this to be particularly noted. Admitting for argument, that *to a certain extent* Dr. W. has expressed himself unhappily, injudiciously and unwisely, in regard to parts of the Psalms—our church is no more responsible for

* For a defense of Dr. W. see Letter XIV.

those forms of utterance which she has never sanctioned, than she is responsible for the blunders of Rouse, in making David say the true Christian in his experience of this life, "hath *perfect* blessedness"—which, of course, is the fruit only of *perfect holiness,* and leads directly to the error of "sinless perfection." So Rouse may have had his *reasons* for exhibiting the Lord Jesus Christ in Ps. 69 : 4, as saying of the satisfaction he made to the Divine law—"TO RENDER FORCED WAS I;" which, of course, utterly subverts the doctrine of Atonement, by representing the blessed Saviour as a *forced victim* to Divine justice! Still, we have too much charity for these brethren, to imagine that they hold these *gross errors,* or that they have ever sanctioned Rouse's *reasons* for so misrepresenting the inspired Psalmist. Let them exercise the same blessed charity toward their brethren of other denominations. We use the poetical labors of Dr. Watts where we approve of them, just as we use those of any other man—but so far and no farther are we responsible for his sentiments. The bitter denunciations he has met with are no concern of ours, except to see that there is no misrepresentation and slandering of the venerable dead. But of this more hereafter.

In view of the offensive language we have quoted in this Letter, it must sadden every Christian heart to reflect that the followers and friends of a common Saviour should allow themselves to speak thus of one another. There are *better moments,* when even the authors of such harsh expressions, under the sacred impulse, we trust, of a common faith and a common salvation, feel free to speak of us as "a branch of the Calvinistic Presbyterian church, who *are doing much to build up the Lord's cause,* * * * *and in whose prosperity we* (they) *rejoice.*"* This is kind and brotherly, but in strange contrast with other forms of expression from the same general source.

It is not the prerogative of man to judge the motives or "try the heart"—but it should not surprise these

* United Presbyterian, of Cincinnati, August 9, 1849.

brethren if we find ourselves unable to appreciate their *extraordinary zeal* on such a topic as Psalmody. In this we only follow the safe precedent of the Rev. Dr. Pressly, of Allegheny City, who many years ago, having become the pastor of a church in Abbeville, S. C., wrote to Dr. J. M. Mason, his former preceptor, as follows:

"I have some trouble occasionally with *extremely good people*, who have great attachment to what they term the 'good old way,' but which might as fitly be called '*tradition of the elders.*' There are *three* bones of contention which have already been often picked, but yet are not likely to be laid aside till some of our fathers are removed to the land of silence, viz. Is it lawful to omit the observance of a fast preparatory to the Lord's Supper? Is it scriptural to extend our Christian fellowship beyond the limits of our own church? Is it right to use any other than a literal version of David's Psalms in the public praise of God?

"When I inform you that it has been customary, on sacramental occasions, to hear those anathematized who would dare to believe the affirmative on either of these points, you will be prepared to understand somewhat of the spirit which we have to meet."

Again, the same writer, after speaking of "*the unity* of the church as taught in the Epistle to the Ephesians," adds—"*This admitted*, the doctrine of Catholic communion seemed to be an irresistible consequence; and therefore I thought it my duty to utter it," i. e. "the doctrine of Catholic communion."* It need occasion no astonishment in the breasts of these brethren, if the arguments which, at *the date of this letter*, convinced *even a Pressly* of the truth of our principles, should even *to this day* be satisfactory to the mind of the Presbyterian body!

It is stated by Dr. M'Master, in his "Apology for the Book of Psalms,"† that "in the neighborhood of those

* Life of Dr. J. M. Mason, p. 487.

† This is the work alluded to by our correspondent, near the commencement of the Letter.

churches where the compositions of Dr. Watts produced dissatisfaction, the Associate Reformed ministers were *not scrupulous in keeping alive* the discontents that existed. It is no impeachment of their motives," he adds, "when it is stated as a fact, that *they profited* by these discontents. Separation from former connections was *encouraged;* and *by such as separated,* their churches, in various parts of the continent, *were enlarged, and some almost wholly formed.*" Again, the same writer charges the Associate Reformed with "employing this as an instrument of *rending churches and of breaking up former connections,*" p. 87. If these things be true, we indulge the hope, that at least since the union with the Associate church better counsels will prevail; and that as branches of the great Presbyterian family, and especially as children of a common Parent, the redeemed of a common Ransom, we shall henceforth coöperate, as far as we can, in the glorious cause of a common Salvation. A spirit such as this will do much to soften asperities, and especially to frown down that disposition, too prevalent among these brethren, to exaggerate, caricature and render odious some of the usages of the Presbyterian church. With the sincere desire to contribute something to the attainment of these much wished for results, the writer has prepared the following Letters. And he has been the more encouraged to this from the fact, that in their "Testimony" these brethren earnestly "beseech us *seriously to consider* the grounds of their controversy with us—and to give them our *prayerful consideration.*"*

The plan proposed in the following discussion is this:

I. To examine the question, whether our brethren employ in praise, "*the songs of inspiration,*" "an inspired Psalmody"—or rather, whether their Psalmody be not, to a great extent, an *explanatory paraphrase.* Letters II.—V.

II. The question of a DIVINE WARRANT for the *exclusive use* of the "book of Psalms," as the only and

* See their Testimony, pp. 7, 46.

perpetual Psalmody of the church, under both Jewish and Christian dispensations, and to the end of time. Letters VI.—VIII.

III. "The more excellent way." Statement and defense of the principles and practice of the Presbyterian church in regard to the subject of Psalmody. Letters IX.—XIII.

IV. Defense of Dr. Watts, &c. Letter XIV.

LETTER II.

QUESTION AT ISSUE: "IS A FAIR AND FULL VERSION" OF DIVINE APPOINTMENT?—ROUSE'S VERSIFICATION NOT "THE WORD OF GOD"—NOT A "VERSION" AT ALL, BUT IN MANY PARTS A "PARAPHRASE," OR MIXTURE OF INSPIRED TRUTH WITH "HUMAN COMPOSITION"—PROVED BY EXTENDED QUOTATIONS.

MY DEAR SIR:—In all discussions of a moral and religious character, it is of the last importance to commence with a well defined statement of the main point in dispute. In arriving at correct views of this subject, we will first present *"the question"* as stated by our brethren, and then point out its inaccuracies and inconsistencies. In some future Letters it will come in course to exhibit *the theory* held by our church, and to defend it against their assaults.

"The *question* at issue," we are told, "is, shall we have any *fair and full version* of this Divine book (of Psalms) as the matter of praise"—or "shall *we reject* that (Psalm book) which God has given, and prefer our own effusions."* "You (Presbyterians) think this heavenly hymn book * * * is obsolete now, and that almost any body can write a *better Psalter* than it is."

* Apology, p. 92. On p. 121, Rouse is called "a *literal and faithful* version."

"Hence you *throw it all away* except *two short hymns*, and substitute in its place *all kinds* of poetry written by all kinds of men." * "The question," we are further told, "has been pressed upon us, involving *an impious rejection* of the Psalms which God has given to his church *as unfit* to be sung, and *the substitution* of hymns of man's composure, &c." †

It would be easy to quote much more of the same sort from the accredited writings of these brethren. But it seems scarcely credible that they really consider the foregoing a fair, unexceptionable statement of the Psalmody question. Certainly they must have known that to the mind of every intelligent Presbyterian it would present only an offensive *caricature*—and that all their arguments to overthrow such positions as those imputed to us, would be viewed by us as "contending with a man of straw," and demolishing a logical figment! and more than this—their statements do not give a correct representation of the position practically held by their authors themselves, as we proceed to demonstrate by incontrovertible facts.

The main proposition of the earliest and perhaps the *ablest* work on the subject, is stated as follows:

"A CORRECT AND FAITHFUL VERSION OF THE WHOLE BOOK OF PSALMS SHOULD BE EMPLOYED IN THE PSALMODY OF THE CHURCH." ‡

This position is vindicated "on the ground of *Divine appointment*"—and heavy judgments are more than *hinted* as the inevitable doom of those who "by their compositions have excluded the *songs of inspiration* from the Psalmody of the church"—and who have preferred "some one prepared by men, to the book of hymns which God has provided." || And much zeal is at times enkindled against this "*profane exclusion* of God's Psalm book!"

* United Presbyterian, of Cincinnati.
† Rev. Dr. Kerr, in Preacher.
‡ Apology, p. 98. The capital letters are not ours.
|| Preacher, June 4th, 1844.

These and many similar expressions of indignation are uttered by those who employ in public and private praise, what is commonly known as "Rouse's version of the Psalms." Of course these brethren must regard that "version" as the *veritable Psalms* of the Holy Scriptures. Hence we are told that "*like the prose version of the Bible,* it is remarkably *literal*—it presents the Psalms in their *native simplicity, beauties and force.*" "We do not say it is perfect; it is susceptible of improvement as the (prose) version of the Bible is"—"it is a *literal and true version.*" *

To the same effect another leading author writes as follows: he is speaking of those who from the very frequent use of the term "paraphrase" in the acts of the Scottish General Assembly authorizing "Rouse's version," "have endeavored to *produee the impression* that it (the "version") was not adopted by those who regarded it as *a literal* or correct translation of the original." Dr. P. adds—"This is disingenuous." Again, Dr. P. tells us, "it (the "version") was adopted upon the principle that it is a faithful translation of the original text." Again, the same writer quotes with strong approval the Rev. Wm. Romaine, affirming that "Dr. Watts had taken *precedence* of the Holy Ghost and thrust him entirely out the church."

Again says Dr. Pressly:—"This (Rouse's) version is not an explanation, but a *translation* of the Psalms. *Like the prose translation* of the whole Bible, it is the work of man, and in some respects might be amended. The *same* will be universally admitted in relation to the prose translation of the Bible. Both these translations are substantially correct and faithful; and for the same reason they are BOTH TO BE REGARDED AS THE WORD OF GOD."

In these extracts from two of the leading authors on that side of the controversy, we have at a glance the precise position maintained by the denominations which

* Apology, p. 121, &c.

they represent; they sing "the inspired Psalm book"—"the word of God;" we sing only "human compositions"—"the effusions of fallible men." Theirs is "God's Psalter"—"a correct and faithful translation;" ours is "a human Psalm book." Their principle is "a *literal* or correct translation." Ours is "human composition" in preference to that of the Holy Spirit.

Now we do not ask the reader to receive our assertions as proof—we appeal to *the record,* and undertake to show by most incontrovertible evidence, that these charges and allegations are without foundation. The Psalmist says, that on one occasion he spoke "in haste"—and so with these brethren in this instance. We accept *the test* which they offer, viz. "the prose translation of the Bible," and we undertake to prove that measured by this rule, "Rouse's version" is not "a correct and faithful version or translation," and is not "for the same reason the word of God." *

And we feel the greater willingness to measure their Psalmody by *this standard,* because in the judgment of the Christian world wherever the English Bible is read, its *fidelity, perspicuity* and excellence have deservedly secured for our prose version a high and distinguished place. "It is the best translation in the world." "It may justly contend with any now extant in Europe." "It is the best standard of our language." "It has enriched and adorned our language." "Of all versions, it must in general be accounted the most excellent." "The translators have seized the very spirit and *soul of the original,* and expressed this almost every where with pathos and energy." "They have been *as literal as they could* to avoid obscurity." Such are a few of the expressed opinions of scholars of the highest eminence, and of various shades of theological belief. And tried by this standard, the system of praise called "Rouse's version" has no just claims to be "a true and literal translation," "or inspired Psalmody"—but to a

* Preacher, Dec. 13, 1844; Aug. 9, 1844.

great extent is a mere patchwork paraphrase, "a human *explanation* of the word of God!" Now for the proof.

We begin with Psalm 102:

PROSE VERSION.	ROUSE.
I am like a pelican in the wilderness.	Like pelican in wilderness *Forsaken I have been.*
I am like an owl of the desert.	I like an owl in desert am, *That nightly there doth moan.*
Because of thine indignation and thy wrath.	Thy wrath and indignation *Did cause this grief and pain.*
And not despise their prayer.	Their prayer will he not despise, *By him it shall be heard.*
When the people are gathered together.	When as the people gather shall *In troops with one accord.*
They that are mad against me, are sworn against me.	The madmen are against me sworn, *The men against me that rose.*
But thou, O Lord, shalt endure for ever.	But thou, O Lord, shalt still endure, *From change and all mutation free.*

These illustrations occur in the first *twelve* verses of the Psalm; and it will be seen that a full half is "mere human composition!" And is this "a literal and faithful version?" Does this "deserve to be regarded as the word of God as really as the prose translation?" Is not this "human explanation?"

We next refer to the 105th Psalm:

PROSE VERSION.	ROUSE.
Seek the Lord and his strength, seek his face evermore.	The Lord *almighty,* and his strength, *With steadfast hearts seek ye:* *His blessed and his gracious* face Seek ye continually.
When they went from one nation to another, from one kingdom to another.	While yet they went from land to land, *Without a sure abode;* And *while,* thro' sundry kingdoms, *they* *Did wander far abroad.*
He sent a man before them.	But yet he sent a man before, *By whom they should be fed.*
Until the time that his word came.	Until the time that his word came *To give him liberty.*

It will be observed that *more than half* of these six

couplets is "mere explanation" and paraphrase. Yet it is all declared to be "not an explanation, but a translation;" yea, a "literal and faithful translation!" Thus "the productions of men are exalted to a level with the word of God!" If this is what they mean by "the songs composed in heaven," which *they profess to sing*, they reduce the inspired word of God very near to a level with their prayers and sermons, "mere human effusions." It would be easy to fill pages with similar illustrations—but lest we should weary the reader, we adduce some further examples under three distinct heads, as follows:

I. In numerous examples, "the human composition" is a mere *repetition* of the inspired sentiment, with some expansion of the thought:

PROSE VERSION.	ROUSE.
How amiable are thy tabernacles, O Lord of hosts.	How lovely is thy dwelling place O Lord of hosts, *to me!* *The tabernacles of thy grace,* *How pleasant, Lord, they be.*
Thy mercy held me up.	Thy mercy held me up, O Lord— *Thy goodness did me stay.*
Round about their habitations.	All round about the tabernacles, *And tents where they did dwell.*
The voice of thy thunder was in the heaven.	Thy thunder's voice along the heaven *A mighty noise did make.*
Thou leddest thy people like a flock by the hand of Moses and Aaron.	Thy people thou didst *safely* lead, Like to a flock *of sheep,* By Moses' hand and Aaron's *thou* *Didst them conduct and keep.*

These are bright specimens of the "inspired Psalmody" of these brethren! "In the Psalms," says one of these authors, "God has presented his own truth in the way which to his infinite wisdom seemed best." But here there is an evident and great departure from "the way of infinite wisdom!" Yet we are required to receive all these "vain repetitions" and *explanations* as "a literal and correct translation of the original."* It is all "the word of God!" With about the same propriety might

* Preacher, December 13, 1844.

they call their pulpit "explanations" of the Psalms "*the word of God!*"

II. Many scores of these "human explanations" are merely Rouse's additional thoughts employed to fill up the verse and make metre. Thus:

PROSE VERSION.	ROUSE.
Be thankful unto Him and bless his name.	Praise, laud and bless his name always; *For it is seemly so to do.*
Which sing among the branches.	Which do among the branches sing *With delectation.*
God hath spoken in his holiness.	God in his holiness hath said, *Herein I will take pleasure.*
My soul breaketh for the longing that it hath.	My soul within me breaks, *and doth* *Much fainting still endure.*
I delayed not.	I did not stay, *nor linger long,* *As those that slothful are.*
I thought on my ways.	I thought upon my *former* ways *And did my life well try.*
For I am become like a bottle in the smoke.	For like a bottle I'm become, That in the smoke is set. *I'm black and parched with grief.*
Their heart is as fat as grease.	Their hearts, *through worldly ease wealth,* As fat as grease they be.

In the following examples Rouse's *explanations* are in italics, to distinguish them from the inspired word of God

Thy *holy* words forgotten have,
And do thy laws despise.

Rose up in wrath
To make of us their prey.

And as fierce floods,
Before them all things drown.

Unto their teeth
And bloody cruelty.

To him that Egypt smote,
Who did his message scorn,
And in his anger hot
Did kill all their first born.

Even through the desert *dry*
And in that place them fed.

To thee *my help alone*
For thou well understands
All my complaint and moan.

Ev'n there they were afraid, and *stood*
With trembling, all dismay'd,
Whereas there was no cause at all
Why they should be afraid.

To learn thy wisdom *and thy truth,*
That we may live thereby.

But overwhelmed *and lost*
Was *proud king* Pharaoh,
With *all* his *mighty host,*
And chariots also.

No comment is necessary to point out to every intelligent reader the absurdity of calling all this "the word of God"—"songs of inspiration;" "songs composed in heaven;" "a correct, faithful and literal translation!" We are almost tempted to employ the language of the prophet, and say of these brethren, "who is *blind* as my servant!" This "THE WORD OF GOD for the same reason that the prose *in our Bibles is so!*"

III. A third class of these "human improvements" includes a full half of Rouse's *inventions*, as follows:

Thou art the God that wonders dost
By thy right hand most strong.

Their ensigns they set up for signs
Of triumph thee before.

A man was famous *and was had*
In estimation.

They set their mouths against the heavens
In their blasphemous talk.

And they a passage had,
Ev'n marching through the flood on foot.

Surely when floods of waters great
Do swell up to the brim,
They shall not overwhelm his soul,
Nor once come nigh to him.

The Lord will light my candle so
That it shall shine full bright.

For in their heart they tempted God,
And speaking with mistrust.

The nations of Canaan
By his Almighty hand.

And there were none to bury them
When they were slain and dead.

So that all passengers do pluck
And make of her a prey.

They in their hands shall bear thee up,
Still waiting thee upon.

The italics will show at a glance where the *inspired* word ends, and Rouse begins his *composition.* We have no room for further illustrations of this sort. But how many of these *complete lines* of Rouse's composition does any one suppose are found in this "correct and faithful version?" We have not examined the whole, but so far as we have compared the "version" with "the prose in our Bibles," we have marked one hundred and seventy-four entire lines. In other words, there is sufficient of this sort of interpolation, this "human" patchwork upon "the inspired word of God," to make seven whole Psalms of the size of Psalm 1, and more than twenty-four of the size of Psalm 117. These are all "the suggestions of men"—they are "human inventions," with which "the word of God" has been interwoven, explained, the versification lengthened out, &c. Yet all this is recommended as a "literal or correct translation of the original text"—"a correct and faithful version," &c.

And now in closing this letter, we make our appeal to every intelligent mind. Are these "the Holy Spirit's Psalms?" Is it not an insult to the Spirit of inspiration to attribute to Him all these specimens of "human effusion." What sort of idea of "inspiration" must they have, who thus degrade it to the level of "human inventions." The theory of "a literal and faithful version as of Divine appointment," proves to be a mere figment. Yet strange to say, these brethren proclaim, "we *dare not* put *a human explanation* in the place of the word of God." "Why does any one ask us to take a human explanation of an inspired Psalm? * * * To such a request we could not accede without offering *criminal disrespect* to the word of God!"* It may perhaps appear harsh to pronounce such professions as these mere oratorical flourishes employed for effect. But facts are stubborn things. We shall resume the subject in our next letter.

LETTER III.

DISCUSSION CONTINUED — ROUSE A PATCHWORK OF HUMAN AND DIVINE SENTIMENTS AND PHRASEOLOGY — NOT THE WORD OF GOD IN THE SAME SENSE IN WHICH OUR PROSE TRANSLATION IS SO — FURTHER EXTRACTS AND PARALLELS TO PROVE THIS.

MY DEAR SIR:—We are employed in testing "the inspired Psalmody" of our brethren, by the *standard* proposed by themselves, viz. the admirably correct and faithful translation found in our Bibles. Do they employ in praise "an inspired Psalmody exclusively?" This is their profession—but we appeal to the record. Our examples have thus far been confined to *complete lines* of interpolation, the *inventions* of Rouse. Let us next glance at some lesser *improvements* upon the inspired text.

Of these smaller additions we have marked more than *three hundred*, varying from a couple of words to almost a full line of the verse. These are all mere human patchwork mingled with the inspired text, and they make "Rouse's version" very unlike "the prose translation of the Bible," and for that reason, it is not "the word of God" in the same sense. We confine our extracts to select specimens, the "*human composition*" being in italics:

Yea thou thine hand dost open wide
And every thing dost satisfy
That lives, *and doth on earth abide,*
Of thy great liberality.

* Pressly on Psalmody, p. 115.

And *divers kinds of filthy* frogs
He sent them to destroy.

Behold the sparrow findeth *out*
A house *wherein to rest:*
The swallow also for herself
Hath *purchased* a nest.

Also the rain *that falleth down*
The pools with water fills.

Who by *assured confidence*
On thee alone doth rest.

And in old age *when others fade,*
They fruit still forth shall bring.

They shall be fat *and full of sap,*
And aye be flourishing.

Although they curse with spite, yet Lord
Bless thou *with loving voice.*

Wherefore their days in vanity
He did consume *and waste;*
And *by his wrath,* their *wretched years*
Away in trouble *past.*

O *Lord, the* God of Israel,
Let none, *who search do make*
And seek thee, be *at any time*
Confounded for my sake.

In the "inspired Psalmody" of these brethren, we have noted three hundred and thirty-two examples of this sort. Varying from *two* words to *six* or *seven,* we will suppose the average to be *three,* which will give one hundred and sixty-six full lines of poetry, the whole of which is "human composition," superadded and interwoven with "the prose translation of the Bible."

Thus taken collectively, we have here matter amounting to seven more full songs of praise of the size of Psalm 1, and more than twenty-four of the size of Psalm 117, all of which is of human origin and invention; yet are we seriously assured by these brethren, that "like the version of the Bible, this of the Psalms is *very literal.*" And Dr. P. adds, "that like the prose version of the Bible, it should be considered as a literal or correct translation of the original text."

In addition to all this, the statements of these authors is

refuted in nearly every page of their Psalmody. Besides matter sufficient to make more than fourteen songs of praise of the size of Psalm 1, and twenty-four like Psalm 117, there is a large number of epithets and expletives of various sorts and sizes, thrown in to fill out the verse, of which we have counted one hundred and eighty-six which belong not to "the prose translation of the Bible." In proof of these allegations we refer *first* to the very *doubtful use* which is often made in Rouse's Psalmody of the peculiar names and titles of the Divine Being as mere verbal *expletives*, mere poetical expedients to round a stanza, or fill up a defective line, where those awful names are entirely wanting in the original. We present the following example, the words supplied being in italics:

The spearmen's host, the multitude
Of bulls, *which fiercely look.*
Those calves which people have *forth sent,*
O Lord our God, rebuke,
Till every one submit himself
And silver pieces bring.
The people that delight in war
Disperse, *O God and King.*

The verse (Ps. 68 : 30) of which this is assumed to be "a literal and faithful version," does not once name the great Being who is the object of all religious adoration; and it really presents a serious inquiry how far this interpolation of the great and glorious NAME which is above every name, for such a purpose, is a *religious* and *devout* use of it—how far it is morally right to thrust these awful titles into the verse to make rhyme, or help out a defective stanza, where Divine Wisdom has seen fit to withhold them; and this objection lies with peculiar force when this is viewed as an irreverent *liberty* taken by "*adding to* the word of God," the very thoughts and matter in which He has "*taught us how to praise,*" thus much and no more. Yet this use of the peculiar names and titles of the Deity is very frequent, not less than eighteen or twenty such examples being found in the 119th Psalm as versified by Rouse; and indeed they are to be thus met with in very many of the Psalms, perhaps in most of them.

The following examples are from Psalm 119:

> An end of all perfection
> Here have I seen, *O God.*
> But as for thy commandment,
> It is exceeding broad.
>
> I am with sore affliction
> Even overwhelmed, *O Lord,*
> *In mercy raise and* quicken me
> According to thy word.

In the *next place,* a similar use is made of many of the revealed perfections of the great and terrible God, for *the mere purposes of poetry,* smoothing a line or completing the requisite number of feet. Such are "Most High," "Most Gracious," "the Eternal," "Mighty," "Almighty," &c. These are all the *improvements* of Rouse upon "the Psalms which God has given." They belong not to the work of the Holy Spirit, but are the work of man.

In the *third place,* there are many scores of adjectives and similar qualifying terms thrown in, and put where the Holy Spirit *never put them;* such as *bashful,* dreadful, bright, clear, glorious, gloriously, sharply, closed, subtilely, wrong, spitefully, wholly, fierce, fiercely, cheerfully, plenteously, devouring, lofty, cruel, sore, safely, faintly, openly, proud, flaming, beloved, dear, truly, continually, dolefully, exceedingly, malicious, greatly, secretly, openly, lewd, mournfully, profanely, pure, untainted, unspotted, sweet, straight, divine, earnestly, carefully, devouring, perplexedly, perfect, and many others of the same sort. These, in the places from which we have copied them, are examples of mere *poetical* license—mere patchwork—"human inventions" to save the credit of the verse, lest it should appear like "the legs of the lame." Of course, they are no part of "the word of God," and therefore form another large collection of exceptions to "the literal or correct translation." Again, we appeal to every candid mind, whether it be a fair statement to speak of such a system of Psalmody as "the inspired Psalter"—"God's Psalm book"—"the songs of the Holy Spirit," &c. Have they not spoken "in haste," who claim for Rouse's version an inspired literalness and correctness equal to the prose translation of the whole word of God? Yet we are told with all possible gravity, that in "these songs the church is furnished with *suitable matter* for praising God, * * * *such matter* as is proper to be offered in praise to God, * * * *the songs* in which He has presented his own truth *in the way which to him seemed best.*"* And to give point and energy to these statements, it is vehemently inquired, "May we not introduce *some things* into the worship of God for which we have not, Thus saith the Lord?" To which I answer, No!† We would respectfully inquire, whether all these *patches* of "human composition" are not "*some things?*" and if so, have they a "thus saith the Lord?"

"Our plea," say these brethren, "is for a *true version* of the book of Psalms as of Divine authority." "An inspired Psalmody only is to be used, to the exclusion of the compositions of men, which *give human views of Divine truth.*"‡ From this it might be inferred that Rouse has not given "human views of Divine truth." Indeed, if "the book of Psalms in a *fair and full version*, a *literal* and faithful version, is alone of Divine authority," as we are assured, then it follows that these brethren use only a human Psalmody! Their "worship is without Divine appointment."‖ In their own language, we say—"these are not the songs which God has given to his church;" but a system as different as a piece of silk cloth patched with more than five hundred fragments of cotton is different from the pure fabric! If a strict literal adherence to the thought, sentiment and order of the Psalms is alone of Divine requirement, then these brethren use a

* Pressly on Psalmody, p. 115.
† United Presbyterian, of Cincinnati.
‡ Pressly on Psalmody, p. 69.
‖ Apology, p. 103.

system of human origin. It would be easy to quote from their volume of praise, many pages of these "*human* views of Divine truth," which they so zealously denounce and so constantly sing! We have space, however, for only a few additional examples, from Psalm 18.

PROSE VERSION.	ROUSE.
I was also upright before him.	*Sincere before him was my heart,* With him upright was I.
Thou wilt save the afflicted people.	For thou wilt the afflicted save, *In grief that low do lie.*
For thou wilt light my candle.	The Lord will light my candle so, *That it shall shine full bright.*
By thee I have run through a troop.	By thee through troops of men I break *And them discomfit all.*

We respectfully submit, that in these and many other similar specimens, for which we have not room, "human views" constitute *more than half* of what is called "a fair and literal version," "an inspired Psalmody exclusively!" And in view of such facts as these, may we not retort upon these brethren the inquiry, "Is not your own Psalmody a presumptuous attempt to improve the work of God?" * Is it thus you treat "those Divine hymns in which you are taught by infinite wisdom *how* to praise Him?"†

Before closing this letter we wish to notice a paragraph from Dr. Junkin's work "on the Prophecies," which these brethren often quote in this discussion with great apparent satisfaction. "Dr. Watts," says Dr. J., "has attempted to improve upon the very sentiment and matter and order of the Psalms." Again, "God's *order* of thought is doubtless the best for his church." Now suppose we grant what is here asserted, does not Rouse alter the *matter and order* and sentiment of the Psalms? Look at the specimens in previous pages! Is there no attempt to *improve* upon the sentiment there? No change

* Preacher, April 5th, 1844.
† Preacher, March 8th, 1844.

of *order?* Take a few specimens in which Rouse inverts the Divine order:

PROSE VERSION.	ROUSE.
Hide thy face from my sins and blot out all mine iniquities.	All mine iniquities blot out, Thy face hide from my sins.
Every one of them is gone backward, they are altogether become filthy.	They altogether filthy are, They all are backward gone.
In God have I put my trust; I will not fear what man can do unto me.	I will not fear what flesh can do, My trust is *in the Lord.*
They have prepared a net for my steps; my soul is bowed down.	My soul's bound down; for they a net Have laid my steps to snare.
God will save Zion, and build the cities of Judah.	For God will Judah's cities build, And he will Sion save.

In the Psalmody of these brethren, there are from forty to fifty such inversions of "God's order of thought." Of course the *crime* in the one case is not less than in the other. Rouse and Dr. Watts are in the same condemnation. Dr. Watts, for example, transposed a part of the verses of Psalm 119, "in order to attain some degree of connection." This was done in a Psalm of which the pious Matthew Henry says, "there is seldom *any coherence* among the verses." There was therefore some excuse for Dr. Watts in changing "the order" of the original—but these brethren reverse "God's order of thought" where there is no such apology, nor *any other*, except that it is so in the "version!" Let common sense decide which is the more guilty party.

But in view of such transpositions as these, perhaps they can inform us whether the "mind of the Spirit is exhibited *so awkwardly* as to render it necessary that the verses should be much transposed."*

We here close our strictures on *the additions* sanctioned and sung by these brethren, upon "the songs which God has given to his church." If we had no further proof, this would suffice to show that the principle which re-

* Pressly on Psalmody, p. 114.

quires a "correct and faithful *version* of the whole book of Psalms, as of Divine appointment," is the merest figment of the human brain. But to make assurance doubly sure, we propose in our next Letter to demonstrate that these brethren are guilty of *numerous omissions* from "the songs in which God has taught us how to praise," "from the *very matter* in which he has presented his own truth *in the way* which to him seemed best." * We shall thus more fully test the professions of these brethren, viz. that "like the prose version of the Bible, their Psalmody is *the word of God.*" Suppose that any man or set of men should publish the whole Bible with such comments, explanations and other human patchwork as the foregoing specimens from Rouse, would any person venture seriously to offer such commixture as the pure Scriptures, the genuine "productions of the Holy Spirit?" Let reason decide.

LETTER IV.

BOOK OF PSALMS NOT DESIGNED TO BE THE ONLY PERPETUAL AND UNCHANGEABLE PSALMODY OF THE CHURCH — NOT SO REGARDED BY THE CHURCH OF SCOTLAND, HER MARTYRS AND HOLY MEN — "A MODERN DISCOVERY" — NOT PRACTICALLY ADOPTED BY THESE BRETHREN THEMSELVES — OMISSION OF PSALM 72 : 20 — MOST OF THE INSPIRED TITLES EXCLUDED FROM ROUSE — THESE PROVED TO BE A PART OF THE INSPIRED TEXT BY DR. ALEXANDER, HORNE AND OTHERS — A GLANCE AT THE PRESBYTERIAN THEORY OF PSALMODY.

My Dear Sir :—The theory of Psalmody taught by the writers we have so often quoted is this: The book of Psalms was designed by its all-wise Author as the unchangeable, all-sufficient and perpetual system of praise, composed for this express object, and of course perfectly adapted to this end. Hence, they infer, to take from or

* Preacher, June 14th, 1844.

to add to this, which is "God's Psalm book"—in other words, to treat it as anything but a *complete and perfect system of praise* for New Testament times, is a species of impiety! Not less so than to *cut out* a part of the Bible, or attempt to *improve*, by additions or otherwise, any other part of the canon of Divine revelation.

That we have fairly stated their views is plain. "Do you think," inquires one, "that the word of God has been given in such a defective form that some parts of it may be *laid aside as useless*, while portions may be selected, &c."* He is arguing against *the omission* of any part of the Psalms, and calls such omission "*laying aside as useless* parts of the word of God."

"The book of Psalms," adds another, "was given as a part of Divine revelation, * * given to the church as *the matter* of her Psalmody." "To take away from its appointed use any portion of sacred Scripture is tantamount to taking it from the Bible." And to enforce this view, he quotes several texts such as these—"Add thou not unto his words, lest he reprove thee and thou be found *a liar.*" "If any man shall take away from the words of this book, God shall take away his part out of the book of life."†

These extracts show with sufficient clearness the precise position of these brethren, and the great marvel is, that they seem never *to have suspected* that they were recording *their own doom!* We have proved in previous Letters, that *adding to* the matter of the Psalms is their habitual practice—that their system embraces many large patches of "human composition." And we are now about to prove that "*they lay aside as useless* large portions of the word of God;" in other words, they *omit* parts of the Psalms from their system of praise.

But before proceeding to the proof, we premise one or two observations:

1. This notion of the absolute and intangible sacred-

* Pressly on Psalmody, p. 112.
† Apology, pp. 101, 116.

ness of the book of Psalms as *the* system of praise for the church in all ages, is purely a *modern discovery!*

The fearful crime of *adding to and taking* away from the book of life, viz. by omitting to use "a faithful and literal version of the Psalms"—seems never to have suggested itself to the church of Scotland in her earliest and best days. Take for example the 51st Psalm, sung by the martyr Wishart, shortly before he suffered death.* As it stands in our Bibles, it consists of nineteen verses and fifty-three lines: as sung by Wishart there are *twenty* verses and one hundred and forty lines. Here is verse 7: "Purge me with hyssop, and I shall be clean; wash me, and I shall be whiter than snow." The martyr sung it as follows:

This isope is humility,
Right law intill ascence.
The snaw sa white in all degree
Betokens Innocence.
For an this twa do govern me
I shall do nane offence.
To thy mercy will I go.

The whole *nineteen* verses are paraphrased in this style—the which, if found in the Presbyterian Psalmody, would be denounced as exposing its authors to a degree of impiety little short of that of "Nadab and Abihu," &c. In truth, as compared with Wishart's broad paraphrase, Dr. Watts has given quite a *close* versification! See Watts' Psalm 51 for the proof.

And when we look into the earliest metre Psalms adopted by the church of Scotland, we are at once struck with the entire absence of anything like "*a fair and literal* version." The versification of Sternhold and Hopkins was introduced, as we are told by Dr. M'Crie in his Life of Knox, "at the establishment of the Reformation," and "was in general use till the time of the Westminster Assembly." Of course, we have only to consult Sternhold and Hopkins to know whether that church adopted the principle of these brethren. That

* See Howie's Scots Worthies, p. 46.

they did not is conceded by all parties. In his report to the Associate Synod on the "improvement of Psalmody,"* Dr. Beveridge, Professor of Theology at Xenia, speaks of Sternhold and Hopkins as follows: "While in *some instances* the adherence to the original is at least as exact as in our present version, in other cases *great liberty has been taken*," and the versification is "far removed from *any thing like* a close translation." Thus we learn from the best authority, that the Psalmody of the church of Scotland in her purest days of reformation, and in the period of her martyrs, was only "IN SOME INSTANCES" as exact in adherence to the original as that by Rouse, while in others it was *no version* at all, "nor any thing like it."

To prove the correctness of Dr. B's. statements, we might cite any number of pages from that ancient Psalmody. For the present, two examples must suffice. The first is in Psalm 125: 1.

PROSE VERSION.	STERNHOLD AND HOPKINS.
They that trust in the Lord, shall be as Mount Zion, which cannot be removed, but abideth forever.	Those who do put their confidence. Upon the Lord *our God only* *And flee to him for their defense* *In all their need and misery:* *Their faith is sure still to endure* *Grounded on Christ the corner stone.* Moved with none ill, but standeth still Steadfast like to the Mount Sion.

A glance will suffice to satisfy any one whether this be "a correct and faithful version or translation!" Yet one of these brethren in his book on Psalmody, calls it "a full version," and quotes others who term it "an excellent translation," and "the word of God!" Thus they place this human paraphrase or explanation on a level with "the word of God!"

Our second example is from Psalm 2: 1, 2.

PROSE VERSION.	STERNHOLD AND HOPKINS.
Why do the heathen rage and the people imagine a vain thing.	Why did the Gentiles *tumults raise* *What rage was in their brain?* Why did the *Jewish* people muse, *Seeing* all *is but* vaine.

* Evangelical Repository, April, 1851.

PROSE VERSION.	STERNHOLD AND HOPKINS.
The kings of the earth set themselves, and the rulers take counsel together, against the Lord, and against his anointed.	The kings and rulers of the earth Conspire *and all are bent* Against the Lord and Christ *his Sonne,* *Which he amongst us sent.*

Now we respectfully submit whether on the principles adopted by our brethren, this be not the grievous crime of "*adding to* the word of God." Observe here the identical *sin* for which they so eloquently denounce our Psalmody, viz. "the gospel turn," by which the Psalmist is represented as speaking of "Christ the corner stone," &c., in the common language of the Christian as distinguished from the Jew!

What floods of ink have been expended in heaping abuse upon Dr. Watts, for the *very thing* which here had the sanction and approbation of the purest church of the Reformation, and in the days of her greatest glory. If these brethren will point out in our system of Psalmody any more gross and *daring* attempt to "convert David into a Christian," viz. "Levitical ceremonies and Hebrew forms of speech changed into the worship of the gospel and *explained* in the language of our time and nation,"* they are welcome to denounce us as *worse* than the Scottish church before the days of the Westminster Assembly. So evident is it that the fundamental principle of our authors is itself a modern "human invention."

2. A second preliminary remark:

These brethren, notwithstanding their harsh language, do not practically adopt their own theory. They do not *act* as though *they believed* us Presbyterians guilty habitually of *crimes* not unlike those of "Uzza, Nadab and Abihu," &c. On the contrary, they often speak of us as a prominent branch of the Christian church, of "intellectual, moral and religious worth, extended activity, great resources and happy influence."† They are always willing to receive the members of our congregations into

* Dr. Watts.

† M'Master's Apology, p. 4.

theirs, nor do they ordinarily require any expression of sorrow for *this sin* of singing hymns, nor a renunciation of private views on the subject, provided they give no trouble. Nay more, they will receive our ministers, though of such *corrupt principles*, and even install them in their *chairs of Theology.** Surely, if these brethren really thought that we Presbyterians had fallen so grievously *under the curse of God*, as their theory teaches, they would not thus deal with us! As to the thousands of eminently pious persons who have "fallen asleep" with the language of our Psalmody on their lips, we leave these brethren to decide what has become of them!

With these preliminary remarks, we proceed to demonstrate certain *omissions* from the "inspired Psalmody."

They have "*laid aside* as useless" the 20th verse of the 72d Psalm: "The prayers of David the son of Jesse are ended." This verse is excluded from Rouse. Nor can it be truly alleged that it does not form a part of the inspired Psalter. There is some difference of opinion among our most eminent Oriental scholars, as to the *relation* which this verse bears to what precedes, whether as the close of the 72d Psalm, or rather as a general *finale* of the second book, or second leading division into which the Psalms have been distinguished. All agree, however, that this verse is a constituent part of the words of inspiration, and of the sacred songs of Zion. It is found in the original Hebrew, in the Greek Septuagint, and in the Latin Vulgate—the two latter of which use, instead of *prayers* of David, the terms *humnoi* and *laudes*—the *hymns* and *praises* of David.

Dr. Addison Alexander, in his "Commentary on the Psalms," thinks it most probable that these words belong "to the *first great subdivision* of the whole collection." As to their relation to the verses immediately preceding, he decides that the verse "forms no part of the 72d Psalm, but relates to the whole series or book preceding."

* The case of Professor Dinwiddie, formerly of Allegheny City, is referred to. He was a colleague of Dr. Pressly.

Dr. A., however, is far from excluding this verse, as Rouse does, from the inspired Psalms. So also the learned Horne, in his "Introduction," gives it as his judgment, that this verse "simply means the Psalms of David in that (the 2d) book," or general division. But he quotes Bishop Horsely as judging it to be "the close of the *particular Psalm* in question, viz. the 72d." "The sense," says Bishop H., "is that David the son of Jesse had nothing to pray for or to wish beyond the great things described in this Psalm. Nothing," adds Bishop H., "can be more *animated* than this conclusion. Having described the blessings of Messiah's reign, he closes with this magnificent doxology:

Blessed be Jehovah God,
God of Israel alone performing wonders;
And blessed be his name of glory,
And let his glory fill the whole earth.
Amen and Amen.
Finished are the prayers of David, the son of Jesse.

Scott, Henry, Poole, and other judicious commentators, agree with this eloquent tribute of Bishop Horsely.

Here, then, on the theory of these brethren, is a plain and inexcusable *mutilation* of the word of God. They have no more right to exclude this verse from "God's Psalm book," than any other verse; and it is equally an "impious license" to lay this verse "aside as useless," as to exclude any other part of the Psalms! Thus they renounce their whole theory as worthless—they treat it with respect only so far as suits their convenience! They expose themselves to the tremendous doom of him who "*taketh away* from the word of life!" No author of eminence has ever questioned the right of this verse to be deemed a component part of the inspired record. By what authority, then, have these brethren ventured to exclude it from the songs which they profess to regard as bearing the great seal of God Almighty as the perfect and perpetual Psalm book of his church, "to which nothing must be added, and from which nothing taken away," under pain of the infinite displeasure of the Author?

Another great omission:

These brethren have "laid aside as useless" most of the titles of the Psalms, which often shed so much light upon their matter. That these inscriptions are of canonical or inspired authority, is fully established by Dr. Alexander. In the preface to his Commentary, he refers to "the strenuous attempts which have been made by *modern writers* to discredit these titles as spurious additions of later date." "These attempts," he adds, "are defeated by the fact that they are found in the Hebrew text, as far as we can trace its history, not as *addenda*, but as *integral parts of the composition*. And such indications of the author and the subject at the commencement of a composition, are familiar both to classical and Oriental usage. That the truth of these inscriptions may in every case be vindicated," &c. And in his note on the title of Psalm 3, he adds, "This is not a mere inscription, *but a part of the text and inseparable from it*, so far as we can trace its history. It was an ancient usage, both among classical and Oriental writers, for the author to introduce his own name into the first sentence of his composition. The titles of the Psalms ought not, therefore, to have been printed in a different type, or as *something added to the text*. In all Hebrew manuscripts," continues Dr. A., "they bear the same relation to the body of the Psalm that the inscriptions in the prophets or in Paul's epistles bear to the substance of the composition." The testimony of this learned and accomplished scholar is summarily as follows:

1. The titles of the Psalms are parts of the inspired text. Yet they are excluded from the Psalmody of these brethren, and thus they "lay aside as useless" a large portion of the songs which God gave to his church.

2. Dr. A. assures us that these titles bear the same relation to the Psalms as the inscriptions in the prophets and in Paul's epistles bear to the writings themselves;

i. e., they belong to the Divine record, were given by the Holy Ghost. Yet they are *rejected* from the Psalmody employed by these brethren.

But we have other testimony. The learned and distinguished Horne, in his "Introduction to the Study of the Scriptures," whilst he candidly admits "that many of the titles prefixed to the Psalms are of very questionable authority, as not being extant *in the Hebrew manuscripts*," yet concedes that we "*have no reason* to suppose that *very many* of them are not canonical parts of the Psalms."* Thus Horne concurs with Alexander, that the titles which "are extant in the best Hebrew manuscripts" are of undoubted canonical authority. Why, then, are they nearly all "laid aside as useless" by those who insist upon "a fair and correct version of the whole book as of Divine appointment!"† Is not this a daring attempt to be wiser than God?

The number of Psalms having titles is one hundred and twenty-five.‡ These inscriptions in the original Hebrew are incorporated in the sacred text, and each title forms a part or the whole of the first sentence or verse of each Psalm. Only *ten* of these titles are versified by Rouse, and the other one hundred and fifteen form a body of inspired matter equal to fifteen songs of praise of the size of Psalm 1, all of which is rejected by these brethren! In all these instances a verse, or part of a verse of "God's Psalm book" is excluded from the position where Infinite Wisdom placed it! And is this the way in which these brethren observe "the Divine appointment of THE WHOLE BOOK to be sung?" From Sabbath to Sabbath they use a mutilated versification of "the Holy Spirit's Psalms!" Would they dare to exclude the inscriptions of Isaiah and Paul? Let any one read the prophecy of Isaiah, omitting the first verse, which Horne says is "the general title of the book" or

* Vol. 4, pp. 105, 106.
† M'Master's Apology.
‡ Horne, vol. 4, p. 105.

let him read the Epistle to the Ephesians, "*laying aside as useless*" the first verse or title, and see what *sad work* it makes with the inspired record! Yet this very thing these brethren do with nearly all the titles of the Psalms. Thus it is obvious that they have adopted a principle in relation to "Divine appointment of the whole book of Psalms," which they *habitually violate* in their practice. Of course, their arguments will have little weight with Presbyterians, until we discover that their practice is in conformity with their settled principles.

It may be supposed that the argument from the omission of the inspired titles, has met with violent opposition. "The title of a song, we are told, and the song itself, are distinct things and for distinct uses; this distinction is well understood and universally observed."* But this is surely a very flimsy sort of argument. "The title of a song and the song itself are distinct things"—very well. The title of a prophecy and the prophecy itself are equally distinct things; and the title of an epistle and the epistle itself are also distinct things. Therefore the practice of including along with the text and reading the title to the prophecy of Isaiah, of which Horne says "the first verse forms the general title," is *an absurd usage!* Isaiah's title should of course be "laid aside as useless!" And so of Paul's epistles. The practice of including the titles contained in the first verses as parts of the epistles, to be *read* as a portion of the inspired text, is also a very absurd thing! We take it for granted, therefore, that when these brethren read the prophecies and epistles, they drop all the inspired titles! This would be treating Isaiah and Paul only as they treat David and others "who spake by the Holy Ghost!"

But it is further objected, that "it is not certain by what authority *many* of the titles were made."* Suppose this to be true, what follows? That *all*, both those which are of undoubted authority, as well as those which are doubtful, must be excluded from the sacred text? Sure-

* Preacher, September, 1852, edited by Dr. Kerr.

ly not. The learned Horne admits that "*some* of them are undoubtedly *not* of equal antiquity with the inspired text" — and the proof is, "they are *not extant in the Hebrew manuscripts.*" Here, then, is a *valid and most safe* test to distinguish the inspired titles from those not of Divine origin. And as Horne further informs us that one hundred and twenty-five of the Psalms have "titles in the Hebrew Scriptures," only twenty-five being without them, is it a good and valid reason for rejecting them all, either to be read or sung, because *some* of them are of "questionable authority?"

Is this a good and sufficient reason for repudiating the whole one hundred and twenty-five titles, as well the few spurious as the many inspired, as "parts of the Psalms!" Truly this evinces most extraordinary respect for the productions of inspiration. Dr. Alexander, however, gives no intimation of such a distinction, but recognizes all the inscriptions as parts of the inspired text, as really as the inscriptions to the prophecies and epistles; and I strongly suspect that Dr. A., who is universally acknowledged to be one of the most profound and accomplished Hebrew scholars in this or any other country, is right, and that Horne is mistaken in this matter.

We have thus the deliberate and well considered judgment of scholars of the highest eminence, affirming that many of the titles are "canonical parts of the Psalms;" and that "*we have no reason* to suppose" the contrary. It follows, therefore, that if "*the whole book* of Psalms is of Divine appointment" to be sung, these brethren *must sing* the canonical titles, or be convicted of *taking away from*, or "*laying aside as useless*," parts of the songs of inspiration.

Not the least curious feature of this whole subject remains to be noticed. It cannot be denied that *Rouse* has embodied in his verse *ten* of the titles of the Psalms. Thus it happens that the very men who treat with the utmost scorn the idea of singing these inscriptions, are *found doing this very thing!* This is clearly proved by the distinguished Horne. He says: "The untitled Psalms in our English version amount to thirty-seven; but *many of these* are Hallelujah Psalms,* which have *lost their inscriptions*, because the venerable translators have rendered the Hebrew word Hallelujah, by the expression, 'Praise the Lord,' *which they have made a part of the Psalm*," &c. From this it appears, that copying the Hebrew original, the translators have embodied the Hebrew titles of "many of the Psalms" in the English version, rendering it, "Praise the Lord." Now what is true of our translation, is also true of Rouse's versification, as any one can see for himself. Hence it follows that these brethren themselves do what they regard as so very absurd, viz. they sing *the titles* of at least *ten* of the Psalms! Horne also says of the Hallelujah Psalms: "To ten Psalms is prefixed the title 'Hallelujah,' which, as already intimated, FORMS PART OF THE FIRST VERSE in our English translation, [and in Rouse's version also,] and is rendered, Praise the Lord." Thus these brethren do the *very thing* which they hold in so much contempt, viz. they sing certain sacred songs, "*commencing with their titles!*" But if it be true, as one writer affirms, that "these titles were *never intended to be sung*;"† then to this extent their worship is without Divine authority! In addition they assume that certain portions (the titles,) of about one hundred psalms, are unsuitable for Divine worship. They presume to exclude and "lay aside as useless" parts of "the songs composed in heaven," and affirm that it is perfectly right to do so. Did our church ever take such strong ground as this?

But in regard to those *titles* which our brethren sing, it has been said that in the original Hebrew, "Hallelujah" "is clearly a part of the Psalm." But this is no more true of the title "Hallelujah," than of all the other

* Horne says the Hallelujah Psalms are: 106, 111, 112, 113, 135, 146, 147, 148, 149, 150.

† Preacher, 1852, by Dr. Kerr.

titles. Every one who can read the Hebrew, knows that this title stands in the precise position toward the Hallelujah Psalms that all the other titles occupy toward their respective songs of praise, i. e. *they stand as part of the first verse*, or compose the whole of it.

We have then the decision of Dr. Alexander, that to omit the titles is "to *mutilate* the sacred text." Tholuck and Hengstenberg take the same ground. These inscriptions existed when the Septuagint was formed, two hundred and eighty years before the Advent, and were even then venerable for antiquity. Kitto receives all of them "except when there is strong *internal evidence* against them."* Indeed the evidence in their favor is so conclusive, that these brethren themselves admit *them as inspired*, except when they are engaged in controversy. Thus a correspondent of one of their leading magazines says: "The titles of the Psalms were written not by the persons who collected them, but by the sacred poets themselves. A similar practice obtained among the ancient Arabian and Syrian poets, of prefixing their names to their songs. The same thing occurs in the writings of the prophets, e. g., the prediction of Balaam, the psalm of Habakkuk, and the song of Hezekiah. Numbers 24, Habakkuk 3, Isaiah 38. That David followed this custom, at least occasionally, is evident from 2 Samuel 22, compared with Psalm 18. We may also with great confidence, refer to him those titles, e. g., Psalms 22, 56, which are poetical in form, and describe the subject of the Psalm."† As to the *suitableness* of the matter of the titles, if that were an open question with these brethren, it would be easy to show that many of these titles are quite as suitable for song as some other parts of the collection. For example, Psalm 102: "a prayer of the

* Biblical Cyclopedia. A high authority adds: "Editorial audacity or ignorance has sometimes gone so far as to omit the titles or inscriptions of the Psalms as forming no part of the text."—*Biblical Repertory*, April, 1859.

† Christian Instructor, edited by Dr. Dales, of Philadelphia, March, 1855.

afflicted, when he is overwhelmed, and poureth out his complaint before the Lord." So also Psalm 18, 51, &c.

We are thus brought to the conclusion, that most of the titles are "inspired portions of the Psalms," originally "composed by the sacred poets themselves." These brethren have incorporated at least *ten* of them in their Psalmody, and they thus recognize them as constituent parts of "the songs composed in heaven," "*the whole book*," which they say is "of Divine appointment" as the unchangeable and perpetual Psalmody of the church. By what authority they venture to "lay aside as useless" the other one hundred and fifteen titles as "not intended to be sung," every one must determine for himself. It will require something more than angry exclamation to prove that they do not, in this thing, lay down their weapons and virtually come over to the Presbyterian camp. The titles which are excluded would form not less than forty-five songs of the size of Psalm 117. How then can they profess to employ "the whole book?"

In conclusion of this Letter, let us glance at the safe position of the Presbyterian church. Our principle, as already intimated, affirms that "the whole word of God is of use to direct us in *praise* as well as in prayer," and that in the New Testament dispensation we are not limited to the precise Psalmody of the Jews in every sentence, line, sentiment, &c.

We maintain that from the rich, abundant and Divine treasures provided by the Head of the church in the book of Psalms and in other portions of the Scriptures, the church, by her highest ecclesiastical authorities, is authorized to select, arrange and introduce all suitable matters for this precious part of Divine worship. We love the book of Psalms, and agree that scarcely any language can be employed too strong and glowing to speak its Divine excellencies and beauties. But we think it no disparagement to say of parts of some of them, a part of the titles for example, that they are not so well suited for Divine worship under the present dispensation as some other parts of Scripture, just as we think scarcely any language too exalted to describe the Divine excellencies of the Bible, which we love and reverence as the text book of the pulpit, and to *be read* in public worship; but there are passages in those Scriptures which no man of common sense would venture to take as his text, or even to *read* from the pulpit! Some texts, for example, in the Levitical law, and which were *read* to the Jews in their worship. Nor is it any reproach to the word of God to say so—because though "all Scripture was given by inspiration of God, and is profitable for doctrine, reproof, instruction in righteousness," &c., yet the several portions were designed by Infinite Wisdom for different uses in the church, and her judicatories and ministers have abundant instruction in the sacred pages themselves, and by the teaching of the Holy Spirit, to guide them aright in the employment of the different portions for their Divinely appointed purposes and objects.

LETTER V.

ROUSE A "PARAPHRASE," NOT A VERSION, OR TRANSLATION — NOT "AS LITERAL AS THE LAWS OF VERSIFICATION WILL ALLOW"— A GLANCE AT THE HISTORY OF SCOTTISH PSALMODY PRIOR TO THE PUBLICATION OF ROUSE — STERNHOLD AND HOPKINS — ITS LOOSE PARAPHRASES AND "GOSPEL TURNS"— THE ACTS OF THE GENERAL ASSEMBLY OF THE CHURCH OF SCOTLAND REPRESENT ROUSE AS A PARAPHRASE — SO CALLED MORE THAN TWENTY TIMES, BUT NOT ONCE A VERSION—VARIOUS OBJECTIONS ANSWERED—CONCLUSIONS—THE REAL QUESTION —"WHETHER SHALL WE SING ROUSE'S PARAPHRASE OR WATTS' PARAPHRASE"— THE PRINCIPLE OF A CORRECT AND FAITHFUL VERSION AS ALONE OF AUTHORITY, A MODERN INVENTION.

MY DEAR SIR:—It has now been demonstrated, if we mistake not, that "the inspired Psalmody" of these brethren, "their literal and faithful version" (or translation) is a patchwork paraphrase, embracing an amount of "the mere effusions of men" sufficiently large to make in the aggregate at least *fifteen* entire "songs of praise" of the size of Psalm 1, and not less than *forty-five* complete Psalms of the size of Psalm 117. Yet all this is in constant use by those who, with the language of fearful warning on their lips, tell us "we have NO AUTHORITY to use the productions of uninspired men!"* All this is dignified with the titles "the Holy Spirit's Psalms," and "*the word of God,* for the same reason that the prose translation of the Bible is the word of God!" This "full and faithful version" (or translation) is affirmed to be imperfect only "as the prose translation is so," &c., &c. Yet where in the "prose translation of the Psalms" can these brethren find one hundred and seventy-four complete lines added to the inspired text? Where will they discover matter and language of "mere human invention" sufficient to compose fifteen whole Psalms such as Psalm 1, or forty-five such as Psalm 117. The thing is impossible, for the whole Protestant world agree

* Pressly on Psalmody, p. 15.

that the English version of the Bible is distinguished for its remarkable literalness, accuracy, and closeness with the Hebrew; and if "susceptible of improvement" at all, it is only as the works of all men are so, from the very nature of man as an imperfect creature.

It has moreover been shown, that by rejecting verse 20 of Psalm 72, along with most of the inspired titles, they "lay aside as useless" a large amount of inspired matter originally indited by the Holy Spirit, and no doubt sung in the worship of the church under a former dispensation. Yet we are assured these brethren sing "inspired songs only," "the book from heaven!"*

The array of facts and quotations in previous Letters, also sheds light upon the question, "Did the church of Scotland, when she authorized 'Rouse's paraphrase,' consider it 'a *literal* and faithful translation?'" If she did, that venerable church certainly made a most singular and unaccountable mistake. If we adopt the views of these brethren, that church gave Rouse their sanction "as a literal or correct translation of the original." "And it is still retained, we are told, because as a *true and literal translation*, it is decidedly superior to *any other* in the English language."† Again, "it is framed on the principle of a translation of the original *as literal* as the laws of versification will allow." ‡

Now these are certainly extraordinary assertions. Take for instance almost any of the examples so readily occurring:

PROSE VERSION.	ROUSE.
But overthrew Pharaoh and his host in the Red Sea.	But overwhelm'd and lost Was proud king Pharaoh, With all his mighty host, And chariots also.

Now can any intelligent person imagine that the church of Scotland really adopted such paraphrases as this with the conviction that they are "a true and literal version or

* United Presbyterian, of Cincinnati.
† Preacher, December 13, 1844.
‡ Pressly on Psalmody, p. 117.

translation—superior to any other in the English language?" Is it conceivable that that venerable church now considers such loose paraphrase "as *literal* as the laws of versification will allow!" * If these brethren cannot frame any more closely literal versification of the foregoing verse, let them go to Dr. Watts, who has it as follows:

> But cruel Pharaoh there
> With all his host he drowned.

So also in verse 10 of the same Psalm:

PROSE VERSION.	ROUSE.
To him that smote Egypt in their first born.	To him that Egypt smote, *Who did his message scorn;* *And in his anger hot* *Did kill all* their first-born.

This is no translation at all, but a broad paraphrase. Dr. Watts has a much more "literal version:"

> He smote their first born sons,
> The flower of Egypt, dead.

These are given as mere specimens, but they are faithful illustrations of the power of prejudice to blind the minds of even good men.†

In the light of many such curious facts as these, we proceed to examine the several acts of the General Assembly of the church of Scotland from 1644 down to 1650, when what is called "Rouse's version" was formally adopted and recommended to "kirks and families." And the first glance at these acts establishes the fact, that they uniformly call Rouse not a *version* (or translation) but only a "paraphrase." In these official decrees we find such phraseology as, "paraphrase of the Psalms"—"new paraphrase"—"our own paraphrase"—"examining and revising the paraphrase"—"considering the English paraphrase"—"authorizing said paraphrase"

* Address, December, 1836.

† In a book just published in Philadelphia by Dr. Cooper and others, they say, "we adhere in our praises to the *very matter* provided for us by Him whose praises we celebrate."—*True Psalmody*, p. 10. Rouse, "*the very matter provided by God!*"

—and finally in 1650, "approving and ordaining said paraphrase, and no other, to be used throughout this kingdom," &c. In these various acts of the Scottish Assembly, the term "paraphrase" is employed not less than *twenty* times, and *not once* is the system called a *version!* Does all this look as though they considered it "a literal and faithful version or translation of the original?" If such men as Alexander Henderson, Rutherford, Gillespie, &c., knew the meaning of their mother tongue, they were surely never guilty of such blunders. In scores of instances a mere school boy could frame a more *literal* yet equally smooth versification.

To weaken the force of this evidence, it has been said that by the term *paraphrase*, the Scottish Assembly meant *version*. No example, however, has been adduced of such a use, or rather *abuse*, of language. Ralph Erskine, who flourished a century and a quarter nearer the period of that Assembly (1649) than we are, may be regarded as good authority on the question. He calls his versification of the Song of Solomon "a paraphrase, or large explicatory poem." Of the nature of his "*version*," one fact is sufficient proof: the title contained in the first line, is paraphrased into *sixteen* lines. And so of all the rest. This was what Ralph Erskine meant by "paraphrase, or *large explicatory poem*."

This should satisfy every candid mind—but even the common standards of the English language teach that "a paraphrase" is a "loose interpretation, an explanation in many words,"* and of course it cannot be the same as "a version or translation." The General Assembly of 1649 well knew what they were saying when they authorized "Rouse's paraphrase of the Psalms with the corrections now given." Most assuredly they could not have meant "a literal and faithful *translation* of the original!"

A rapid glance at the early history of Psalmody in the church of Scotland, will shed some further light upon

* Johnson followed by Walker.

the subject. Prior to 1546 there is no authentic account of metred Psalms. But the Psalms were used *in some form* in Divine worship.* It was in this year (1546) that Scotland's second martyr, the cotemporary, preceptor and friend of John Knox, and to whom Knox "was of all men most indebted," sealed his devotion to his Divine Lord and Master with his blood. On the night when Wishart was apprehended, he gave a most consoling discourse on the death of God's children, and though he knew that on the morrow he should go to the stake, he said, "Methinks I desire to sleep." He then appointed the 51st Psalm to be sung, which had been turned into rhyme, &c.† But was this 51st Psalm "a literal and faithful version?" It has been shown in a previous Letter that the fifty-three lines in our Bibles were expanded into one hundred and forty of "the effusion!" We have room for only one additional stanza.

PROSE VERSION.	WISHART'S HYMN.
Though delightest not in burnt offering.	Burnt sacrifice is no delite Unto thy Majestie— Thou carest not of it one mite For sinne to satisfy. For only Christ did make us quit Of all enormitie. To thy mercie will I go.

This was the form in which the martyrs and early reformers of Scotland sung the Psalms. Those holy men do not seem to have suspected any *crime* in such a *gospel use* of the inspired records. The whole song is in the same style, paraphrase and "gospel turns" after the manner of Dr. Watts! According to our brethren, this was not "practicing Psalmody" at all, but singing "the mere effusions of men."‡

This appears to have been among the earliest "metred

* M'Master's Apology, p. 74.

† Howie's Scots Worthies, p. 46.

‡ Yet Dr. Cooper and others tell us: "The reformers of Scotland neither made hymns nor sung them."—*True Psalmody*, p. 124. This song of Wishart was as much "a *hymn* of human composition" as any Watts ever wrote.

Psalms" in Scotland; but in the southern parts of the island, as far back as 1538, Miles Coverdale (an honored name in the annals of the Reformation,) had made the earliest known attempt at rendering Psalms into English verse for the purposes of sacred song. During the reign of Edward VI. he published "Ghostly Psalms and Spiritual Songes, drawen out of the Holy Scripture." In his preface Coverdale states that he had "set out certain comfortable songs *grounded in God's word*, and taken some out of the Holy Scripture, specially out of the Psalms of David, in order that the youth of England," &c. His book contained only *thirteen* Psalms, viz. the 2d, 11th, 13th, 24th, 45th, 50th, 67th, 123d, 129th, 133d, 136th, 147th, and 127th. The remainder consisted of versifications "*grounded on other parts* of God's word." So early did "*corruption* of Divine worship" begin in that church!*

The versification by Sternhold and Hopkins made its appearance 1549–1563, at which latter period was published "*The whole Boke of Psalmes* collected into English metre, *conferred with the Ebrue*." This was the system of Psalmody used by the church of Scotland for one hundred years before the adoption of that by Rouse. Was it framed on the principle of "a true and literal translation?" Very far from it. Professor Beveridge, as already quoted, admits that it was not. For example, take the last lines of the second Psalm:

PROSE VERSION.	STERNHOLD.
When his wrath is kindled but a little. Blessed are all they that put their trust in him.	If once his wrath never so small Shall kindle in his breast, O then all they trust in Christ Shall happy be and blest.

Here again we find the "*gospel turn*" so frequently used by Dr. Watts! But besides the constant recurrence of broad paraphrase, to the 75th and 125th Psalms are appended "doxologies." The former reads as follows:

* Our authority for these facts is Thomas H. Horne.

To Father, Son, and Holy Ghost,
All glory be therefore:
As in beginning was, is now,
And shall be evermore.

The other is larger, and is without the smallest mark to distinguish it from the body of the Psalm:

Glory to God the Father of might,
And to the Sonne our Saviour,
And to the Holy Ghost, whose light
Shine in our hearts and us succor:
That the right way from day to day
We may walke and him glorifie:
With heart's desire all that are here,
Worship the Lord, and say, Amen.

These are purely "human composures" added to the inspired text, "necessarily defective effusions, claiming no higher origin than the ingenuity of man."* If these brethren, some of them at least, had lived in the days when this Psalmody was used, and had held the same views they now profess, they must have seceded from the Scottish church. They could not have tolerated such "deviations from the appointed order"—such contempt of "a punctilious regard to every part of Divine institutions"—such "intrusion of an unhallowed hand upon the ark of God"—such "impious license"—such "encroachment upon the instituted ordinances of God." They must have issued their "Testimony" against these *daring crimes*, lest they should partake of the sin of "Nadab and Abihu," and fled from a church which by thus "adding to the words of God," must have been "*reproved and found a liar.*" So true is it, that in many points Sternhold and Hopkins' system bears a stronger resemblance to the Presbyterian Psalmody than to "a true and literal version." In a future Letter† some further illustrations of these curious facts will be adduced, in connection with another topic.

Thus, then, from the days of Knox and Wishart down to the period of the Westminster Assembly, the noble

* Apology, p. 202.
† See Letter IX.

apostolic church of Scotland decidedly *condemned* in her practice the principle of "a correct and faithful version of the whole book of Psalms." This of itself is presumption strong against that principle, especially when associated with the arrogant claim of "Divine appointment," which of course places the ban upon all else as "human invention," "will worship," &c.

If the reasonings of these brethren be correct, that venerable church, for the first century and a quarter of her existence, had only a "human Psalmody!" Her martyrs, confessors, and apostolic men, sung in the praise of God only or chiefly "their own effusions," "the imperfect, however well intended, effusions of fallible men," &c.!

If it should be inquired—Why did that venerable church lay aside Sternhold and Hopkins, and adopt that commonly called Rouse's version? we answer in the words of Dr. Beveridge: "In process of time the *change in the English language* became so great, and the dissatisfaction with this *antiquated* version so general, that the necessity of an improved version became evident." But neither Dr. Beveridge nor any other writer that we have ever met with, pretends that the change was made on the ground that the martyr church of Scotland had for a century been guilty of a daring and high handed invasion of the Divine prerogative—had committed a sin resembling the fearful crime of Uzza—had offered in her songs of praise the strange fire of Nadab and Abihu!! There were reasons sufficient, as Dr. Beveridge well observes, occasioned by the lapse of time and the revolution in language, to warrant a change, without resorting to the startling supposition, viz. that the martyr church of Scotland then for the first time awoke to the fearful fact, that for a hundred years and more she had habitually profaned and trampled under foot one of the most precious ordinances of God's house!

The principle of "a correct and faithful version or translation," is thus demonstrated to be a *modern invention!* It is repudiated by the earliest specimens of Psalmody sung by distinguished reformers, martyrs and holy men of God. It is repudiated by the earliest complete versification of the Psalms authorized by that church. It is repudiated by the very system used by these brethren themselves and by the church of Scotland—viz. *Rouse.* The men who framed and introduced it, were familiar with many safe precedents in the Scottish, French and other reformation churches, which gave no countenance to such a principle, but the very reverse. They evidently had no thought of making "a literal translation," as is demonstrated by the title "paraphrase," employed in their solemn ecclesiastical acts; and especially, by examining the "version" itself, nothing can be plainer than that it is very far removed from "a true and literal translation." Those who speak of it under this presuming title, and call it "an inspired Psalmody," are themselves guilty both *of "adding to* and *taking away* from the word of God." To represent this patchwork system as "an inspired Psalmody," is to degrade the productions of the Holy Spirit to a level with the effusions of men!" To represent Rouse's paraphrase as "the Psalms and hymns and spiritual songs *which God has given us in his word,*"* is a gross abuse of language, to say the very least.

Let us now turn to some of the objections or evasions, by which these conclusions are attempted to be set aside:

1. To account for the very paraphrastic character of Sternhold and Hopkins' psalmody, it has been attributed to "the difficulty experienced in that age in making a strict translation." But the work itself refutes this evasion. It gives no explanation at all of the "doxologies" before quoted, which are pure "human composition." Nor does it account for the numerous "gospel turns," paraphrastic and explanatory clauses, &c. &c. No one acquainted with the history of the church of Scotland, her mighty men of stature, her noble army of martyrs, would pay them such an equivocal compliment. It will not do to charge upon that glorious old Presbyterian

* Preacher, February 23, 1844.

church "intrusion of a profane hand upon the ark of God," contempt of "Divine institutions," &c., and then apologize for her crimes, by alleging that she had no minds capable of making as "correct and faithful" a versification as that of Rouse!

These brethren know too well what sort of men constituted the early church of Scotland, and comprehend too accurately the absurdity of such a solution of the difficulties suggested by the examples adduced. Besides, rather than thus "*impiously* corrupt the ordinance of God," why not chant the prose of their Bibles? "In the Scottish church," says one of these authors, "the reformers are reported to have sung the book of Psalms in prose — the form, perhaps, in which it should still be used."* If this be so, then surely that noble old church was under no necessity of *corrupting* the Psalms which God has given! She was not chargeable with the unnatural crime of giving her children a stone, instead of bread—instead of a fish, a scorpion! But besides all this, in many parts *Rouse* is very little better than Sternhold. Thus the difficulty remains in all its force.

2. Admitting the imperfections of "Rouse's version," it is sometimes said: "We are not particular about a *version*, but only contend for the principle of an inspired Psalmody." In other words, your *theory* is very sound, but in practice you trample it under foot! The story is told of one who professed to be a very rigid Calvinist, but was often found intoxicated and profane! When he was reproved by his pastor, he replied: "My dear sir, my principles are perfectly sound, though I admit I pay no regard to them in my life!" Our brethren are very earnest in defending "a true and literal version as of Divine appointment." But as to their practice, that is left to take care of itself; and "Divine appointment" is permitted to "go and do likewise!" We have shown by numerous extracts from their own writings, that whilst constantly employing a patchwork paraphrase, they pro-

* M'Master's Apology.

fess to sing "inspired songs only," "the word of God," &c.* Thus they speak of their Psalmody!

3. It is further objected, that on the original title page, "Rouse's paraphrase" is represented as "more agreeable to the original text than any heretofore"† But this is not denied. Suppose it to be "more agreeable" to the original than "Sternhold and Hopkins"—does that prove it to be "a literal and faithful version?" Is it therefore "the word of God in the same sense with the prose of our Bibles?"

4. It is further objected, that the same original title-page represents "Rouse's paraphrase" as "translated and diligently compared with the original text," &c.† But what does this prove? In order to make a correct paraphrase it is of course indispensable to consult the original text. And as to the use of the term "translated," it proves nothing, especially nothing against the evidence of facts adduced in former letters. Dr. Watts applies the very same term to his "paraphrase." And the original title of Sternhold and Hopkins' contains the clause, "conferred with the Ebrue." But who is now so foolish as to call that system "a true and literal version," or indeed a version at all? The chosen title used by the Scottish General Assembly is "paraphrase." Still we do not deny that in a part of the Psalms, Rouse's is a version which may be properly termed "correct and faithful;" but if *facts* do not deceive, there can be as little doubt that as a system it is not "a literal and faithful version," but in numerous instances, as we have proved, is a paraphrase or explanation. The Psalmody of the Presbyterian church, as arranged by her committees, is *in many of the Psalms,* as *correct a version* as Rouse. Yet the whole is denounced as "the effusions of fallible men," while "the human additions" and "improvements" of Rouse are called "*the word of God!*"

* "If the book of Psalms in the prose translation, deserves to be regarded as *the word of God,* * * * the metrical version *possesses substantially the same character.*" Pressly on Psalmody, p. 117.

† Preacher, December 13th, 1844.

5. It is objected that the Scottish commissioners, Rutherford and Gillespie, in writing to their General Assembly say—"It [Rouse] will be found as near the original as any *paraphrase* in metre can readily be." * We think so too. It would really be a difficult task to construct a *paraphrase* in metre, (observe, a *paraphrase*, not a translation,) much, if at all more near the original than this of Rouse. But does that prove the paraphrase to be "a literal and faithful version," or translation of the original?

6. It may be alleged, that vigorous efforts are now being made to improve the "paraphrase of Rouse," so as to make it "a literal version." We have before us two of these "improved versions," but compared with *Rouse*, they make but small pretensions to be an "inspired Psalmody." We give one or two illustrations. Thus in Psalm 147: 10—"He delighteth not in the strength of the horse; he taketh not pleasure in the legs of a man."

ROUSE.	IMPROVED VERSION.
His pleasure not in horse's strength, Nor in man's legs doth lie.	Not in the fleetness, or the might Of horse or man, can God delight.

So also in Psalm 136: 15—"But overthrew Pharaoh and his host in the Red Sea."

ROUSE.	IMPROVED VERSION.
But overwhelmed and lost Was proud King Pharaoh, With all his mighty host *And chariots also.*	But overwhelmed and lost Was Pharaoh, that proud king, With all his mighty host *Which he did with him bring.*

Both these *versions* "lay aside as useless" the inspired clause "in the Red Sea!" Do these brethren imagine "they *write better than David!*" Again, Psalm 122: 1—"I was glad when they said unto me, Let us go into the house of the Lord."

ROUSE.	IMPROVED VERSION.
I joy'd when to the house of God, Go up, they said to me. Jerusalem, within thy gates Our feet shall standing be.	I was glad to hear them say, *On the holy Sabbath day,* Let us now attend the courts *Where the Holy One resorts.* We within thy gates will stand, Salem, *pride of all the land.*

* Preacher, December 13, 1844.

Where these brethren learned that the Psalmist's *gladness* was "on the holy Sabbath day," more than *any other day*, they do not inform us. Certainly the Psalm does not say so. They seem to have thought they could "*improve* upon David!" Yet they tell us, in their *Preface:* "The principle which the Associate Reformed church holds, is, 'a *faithful translation* or *version* of the book of Psalms!'" And the foregoing are a few out of many scores of examples of this "*faithful translation!*" These are not very promising attempts to obtain a more "true and literal version" than Rouse. Indeed, if *Rouse* was "framed upon the *principle of a translation* of the original as close as the *laws of versification will allow*,"* as Dr. Pressly assures us, it is of course vain to expect any more closely literal system, unless the original authors were totally unqualified for their work, which Dr. P. will not venture to affirm.

And now, what are the fair and legitimate conclusions from this investigation?

1. We have shown, by undeniable facts, that these brethren have *taken away* from "the songs of inspiration, in which God teaches his church *how to praise*,"† an amount of matter equal to forty-five songs of the size of Psalm 117, and that they *have added to* these songs "human composition" to the same amount. Of course their pretensions to "a correct and faithful version" of the whole book, are a nullity.

2. We have proved that the earliest specimens of Psalmody in metre, as used by our Scottish forefathers, sung by their martyrs and reformers, were not formed upon the *literal* principle, but were much more nearly after the style and manner of the Presbyterian system, only much *more* paraphrastic.

3. We have proved that from the period of the establishment of the Reformation down to the Westminster Assembly, that noble Apostolic church employed in pub-

* Address, December, 1836.

† Pressly on Psalmody, p. 118.

lic and private worship a versification of the Psalms (Sternhold and Hopkins') which utterly condemns and repudiates the principle of "a literal and faithful version of the whole book," being in many particulars more like the Presbyterian Psalmody than "a literal version."

4. We have demonstrated by the record itself, that the Psalmody employed in the Presbyterian churches of Scotland (Rouse's paraphrase) ever since the Westminster Assembly, is widely different from a "literal and faithful version or translation of the whole book of Psalms;" so that the authority and example of those venerable churches is with the Presbyterians, rather than with these brethren. And in view of such facts, their denunciations of terrible judgments on the *sin* of singing "human composures," &c., while they habitually do the *same wicked thing*, will be more likely to produce a *smile* than *conviction*—at least with all intelligent Presbyterians.

5. It has been demonstrated that the system of Psalmody called "Rouse's version," is "the word of God" in a sense similar to that in which a piece of cloth interwoven with more than five hundred patches of *cotton* is the *pure silk fabric!* Of course, the lofty claims which are made in its favor appear rather small. And if, as we are assured, *the whole* book of Psalms is of "*Divine appointment*," then these brethren use "a human Psalmody!" Yet they tell us, "our plea is for a true version of the book of Psalms as of Divine authority."* "We sing inspired songs only."

And what shall we say of the rash assertion, that, "like the prose translation of the whole Bible," Rouse "*is to be regarded as the word of God?*" If in the Psalms, or in any other book of the Holy Scriptures, the same amount of such interpolation and comments were found, the whole Protestant world would condemn the translation and call imperatively for a new one. It would not be tolerated at all as "the Bible without note

* Apology, p. vi.

or comment." And yet we are assured, "The question is simply this—shall we use the Psalms and hymns and spiritual *songs which God has given* in his word? Or shall we use such as have been prepared by uninspired men?"*

Again. "The substitution or use * * * * of imitations and *paraphrases*, is *a corruption* of the worship of God!"† Yet these brethren constantly use "Rouse's Paraphrase, or Explanation of the Psalms!" As to the Collections of Hymns employed by nearly all the Scottish churches, Presbyterians may well rejoice to be denounced in company with such men as Drs. Chalmers, Candlish, Duff, and a host of others, in like manner "corrupters of the worship of God!" But we shall speak more fully on this point in another Letter.

* Preacher, February 23, 1844.

† Basis of Union submitted by the Associate or Seceder church to the Associate Reformed church.

LETTER VI.

SOURCES WHENCE SONGS OF PRAISE ARE TO BE DERIVED — PRESBYTERIANS RECEIVE ALL SCRIPTURE AS OF USE TO DIRECT US IN PRAISE AS WELL AS IN PRAYER — OPPOSITE DOCTRINE, THE PSALMS EXCLUSIVELY — ALL BESIDES CORRUPTION OF DIVINE WORSHIP — SCOTTISH CHURCHES GENERALLY USE OTHER SONGS BESIDES THE PSALMS — EXAMPLES, FREE AND ESTABLISHED CHURCHES — UNITED PRESBYTERIAN CHURCH, &C.— OUR BRETHREN REJECT ALL INSPIRED MATTER FOR SONG, EXCEPT ONE HUNDRED AND FIFTY PSALMS — THEIR THEORY NOT SUSTAINED BY THE EXAMPLES OF OLD AND NEW TESTAMENT PROPHETS AND INSPIRED MEN, ISAIAH, HEZEKIAH, &C.

MY DEAR SIR :—We come next to examine the *sources* whence, according to these brethren, the church should derive all her songs of praise.

The doctrine of the Presbyterian church is this: As we are taught in the Westminster Catechism that "the whole word of God is of use to direct us in prayer," so we maintain it to be of "use to direct us" in *praise.* And this view seems the more probable, because in every *other department* of public and private worship, none but the Jews restrict themselves to the Old Testament. Indeed the person who should seriously advise these brethren to limit all other Divine worship to the forms and phraseology of the Jewish Scriptures, would only expose himself to their contempt!

On the other hand, the doctrine taught by these brethren is as follows: "It is the will of God that the sacred songs contained in the book of Psalms be sung in his praise to the end of the world; and we have *no authority* to use any other." Or as otherwise expressed: "It would appear to be the Divine will that this (book of Psalms) should be used to the exclusion of all others."* What these brethren include in the terms "*sacred songs* of the book of Psalms," we learn by their common

* Pressly on Psalmody, p. 87.

usages, viz. such paraphrastic and explanatory versifications as those of Rouse. In their books intended for general circulation — in their arguments with other denominations, and in their formal "Testimony" against the errors of their brethren, "it is for the use of the Psalms in a *faithful translation* they testify."* But when we examine their Psalmody, we are at no loss to decide how far "a correct and faithful translation" governs their practice. It has been abundantly shown in previous Letters, that they sing "a paraphrase," a large mixture of "human composition" with the Divine thought and phraseology; often inverting the *order and arrangement* of "God's Psalm book!"

But the question of the *exclusive use* of the book of Psalms is with these brethren no *mere theory* in other aspects—but one of very great practical importance. "Maintaining as we do," they say, "the exclusive use of that compilation of sacred songs which God *has prepared* and given to his church, we are under *the necessity* of holding those who depart from this appointment, as *seriously corrupting* one of the most interesting and important ordinances of God."† And to enforce this charge of *corruption,* the same writer affirms, that "compared with the prose version of our Bibles," Rouse's versification "is formed on the principle of a *literal* translation!" Of course he holds that he and his brethren sing "a *faithful and literal* translation," which equally with the prose, *is the word of God!*‡

But where do they find Divine authority for restricting the praises of the church under the New Testament to the "book of Psalms?" In solving this question we ask attention to several particulars:

1. The question as stated in the extracts given above, is not the question of "the exclusive use of an inspired Psalmody." Even if Rouse were all that some profess

* Testimony of the United Presbyterian church, p. 46.

† Preacher, by Dr. Kerr, June 9, 1847.

‡ "No argument is needed to prove that Rouse's version is the word of God."—*Dodd's Reply.*

to believe it, viz. "*the very word of God*," (a monstrous assertion,) still the inquiry returns—"are there no inspired Psalms, hymns and songs in other parts of the Bible?" Certainly there are. Well, then, suppose that these *other songs* not found in the book of Psalms, were paraphrased in metre as closely to the original as Rouse, would they from that moment cease to be inspired songs? Do they then become "corruptions of worship" to all that use them in praise? So teaches the theory of our brethren. Thus instead of testifying, as they profess, "for the use of an inspired Psalmody,"* they are found testifying *against* a large number of sacred songs, the productions of the Holy Spirit!

Thus their theory condemns the use of all "inspired compositions," which are not among the one hundred and fifty Psalms. As for example the *sixty-seven* "translations and paraphrases," employed by the Free and Established churches of Scotland. These extend from Genesis to Revelation; and many, perhaps *all* of them, are as close to the Scripture text as many parts of Rouse's paraphrases. Yet while Rouse is vehemently defended as "inspired Psalmody," these other "songs composed in heaven" are mere "corruptions of worship!"

The same line of argument applies to the "hymn book of the United Presbyterian church of Scotland." It contains four hundred and ninety paraphrases of portions of Scripture referred to in the titles of the several hymns, most of which Scriptures are found outside of the Psalms. Many of these are as close paraphrases of Holy Writ as large portions of Rouse. Yet all are "corruptions." It is a mistake, therefore, in these brethren to say: "The principle of which we are the advocate, is the songs of inspiration."† Neither is it "the *great question*," as they affirm, "whether we have authority to use any other than the songs of inspiration." It is demonstrated by your own statements as given above,

* Testimony of United Presbyterian church, p. 46.
† Preacher, by Dr. Pressly, February 23, 1844.

that you *testify* against all the inspired songs of the Bible, except one hundred and fifty Psalms. "These Divine songs," this "collection of Psalms," &c., we are told, "constitute an *inspired system of Psalmody*."* On this exclusive theory, all inspired songs not contained in that "collection," are "corruptions" of Divine worship, if used for purposes of praise! Against all such *they testify*. Thus a large number of "the songs of inspiration" are "laid aside as useless."

2. Our second remark is this: That these exclusive principles are quite unseemly and unnatural among those who strenuously maintain the Divine origin of the whole Bible. It is well known to every student of the Scriptures, that large portions of the prophecies, Job, Proverbs, Solomon's Song, and the Lamentations, (to say nothing of the songs of the New Testament,) are written in the strains of the most sublime and beautiful poetry. Yet all this devotional and inspired matter, though often the very Psalms and songs in which inspired men praised God, and called upon the church to praise him, is utterly discarded by the exclusive doctrine. For example, Isaiah, chapter 5: "Now will I sing to my well beloved *a song* of my beloved," &c. The *beloved* was of course the only true God, and this song was an act of praise to him. Again, chapter 12: "In that day thou shalt say, O Lord I will praise thee; * * * the Lord Jehovah is my strength and my song, and he is become my salvation," &c. "The structure of this Psalm," says Dr. J. A. Alexander, "is very regular."—*Commentary*, p. 237.

The character of Isaiah as the penman of the Holy Ghost, stands among the very highest of the writers of the Scriptures. His very name means "the salvation of Jehovah," and his illustrious predictions of the birth, character, mission, miracles, sufferings, death, burial and final glory of the Messiah, have won him the distinction, "the Evangelical Prophet." His descriptions of the establishment, increase and perfection of

* Pressly on Psalmody, p. 142.

Christ's kingdom on earth, by the effusions of the Holy Spirit, have made his prophecies rather a *fifth gospel* than a series of predictions, a history rather than a vision of the future. The transcendent excellencies of his compositions, at once forcible, elevated, majestic, sublime and highly ornamented, have entitled them justly to the praise of being "the most elegant part of the Old Testament writings;" and won to himself the distinction of being "the Prince of the Old Testament Prophets." Of this 12th chapter, Horne * says: "This hymn seems by its whole tenor, as well as by many of its expressions, *much better* calculated for the use of the Christian than for the Jewish church, * * and the Jews themselves seem to have applied it to the times of the Messiah." Moreover, this highly evangelical Psalm, says Dr. Alexander, "the prophet *puts into the mouth* of Israel," or the church. She is instructed to *sing this song*, though David and Asaph had been in their graves not far from three hundred years; nor does it belong to their system of Psalmody. Of course Isaiah did not adopt the theory which limits the church to "David and Asaph," and two or three others.

Let it be observed, too, that all our best commentators, Henry, Scott, and others, interpret *this song* of the times of the Messiah, ("*in that* day, *the gospel day*, thou shalt say,") and its instructions as eminently applicable to the Christian dispensation. Can it then be a "corruption of worship" to sing such a Divine song as this 12th chapter of Isaiah!

The argument is still more striking in regard to chapter 26. "In that day shall this *song be sung*," &c. Dr. Alexander says, "It is not at all improbable that this song was actually used in praise, as it is written in the form and manner of the Psalms." And he calls it "a song to be sung by Israel," or the church. Henry adds—"In that day, i. e., the gospel day, which the day of the victories and enlargement of the Old Testament

* Introduction, vol. 4, p. 160.

church was typical of. * * * The land of Judah was a figure of the gospel church," &c. Scott expounds to the same effect. The church, therefore, is only fulfilling the predictions of the infallible Word, when she sings such songs as these. She only assumes the character in which she is arrayed by "the sure word of prophecy."

3. It would be easy to adduce scores of similar evangelical Psalms from Isaiah and other prophets, but we cannot enlarge. Before dismissing the subject, however, we must refer to the song of Hezekiah, Isaiah 38 : 9–20. "That Hezekiah should compose a Psalm," remarks Dr. Alexander, "is not strange. * * It would be far more strange if one so much like David in character and spirit had not followed his example." "The inspiration and canonical authority of this production are clear from its incorporation by Isaiah among his prophecies." * It is Hezekiah's Psalm of thanksgiving after recovery from dangerous illness. David and the other Psalmists of his day had been dead for three hundred years; but "by David's instrumentality," we are told, "the church was furnished with a choice variety of Psalms, &c. adapted to the diversified circumstances of *the private believer*, and of the church of God."† What, then, was the obvious duty of Hezekiah? Surely as "a *private believer*" to adopt and sing one of "that collection of sacred songs which were to be used to the exclusion of all others." But this he did not do. Neglecting the "*choice variety*" furnished by "the sweet Psalmist of Israel," he writes *a Psalm for his own use.* And this song, be it observed, has no place in the "book of Psalms."

But Hezekiah did much more than this. In the 20th verse of this same chapter, he says—"The Lord was ready to save me, therefore we will sing *my songs* to the stringed instruments all the days of my life in the house of the Lord." "The phrase 'we will sing,'" remarks Dr. Alexander, "refers to the multitude who might be

* Commentary on Isaiah 38.

† Pressly on Psalmody, p. 79.

7

expected to join in his public thanksgiving, not only at first, *but in after ages.*" "The general sense," he adds, "is that of *public* and *perpetual praise;*" and that "in the house of the Lord"—or as part of the stated public service of the church. How unseemly and unnatural, then, for our brethren, who, we are glad to say it, are *generally sound* on the question of inspiration, to set themselves in hostility to such "inspired songs" as these—songs whose public and private use in the praise of God is sanctioned by the very "Prince of the Prophets." We have presented several specimens taken from a great number of *Divine songs.* They were either written by Isaiah or received his sanction—were designed for the use of the church, and "God's worshiping people under both the old and the new dispensation were directed to sing them." * Yet all are excluded by these brethren! How evident is it, therefore, that their *principle is not* that of an "inspired Psalmody." By their own showing, they select from the inspired volume some Psalms, and reject others—they *testify* in favor of a certain number of inspired songs, and *testify against* a far greater number equally Divine, "equally composed in heaven!" They sing a part—others, they venture "to lay aside as useless."

But perhaps it will be replied, that they have "Divine appointment" of the "book of Psalms" to be used exclusively in New Testament worship; but no such "appointment" for any others, whether inspired or uninspired. This assertion, in both its parts, we propose to examine in our future Letters; when we hope to make it more fully appear that no such Divine warrant exists for the exclusive use of the book of Psalms.

* Testimony of the United Presbyterian Church, p. 44.

LETTER VII.

QUESTION OF "DIVINE APPOINTMENT" OF THE BOOK OF PSALMS EXCLUSIVELY FOR PRAISE—EXAMINATION OF THE USUAL ARGUMENTS—2 CHRON. 29: 30 NO DIVINE WARRANT—PECULIAR CHARACTER OF THE MATTER OF THE PSALMS—THEIR TITLES—THEIR ORIGINAL USE SHOWN TO BE FALLACIOUS AS PROOFS OF PERPETUAL AND UNCHANGEABLE DESIGNATION FOR EXCLUSIVE PRAISE IN THE CHURCH—THE TITLE OF "SOLOMON'S SONG" PRESUMPTIVE PROOF THAT IT SHOULD BE USED FOR PUBLIC PRAISE.

My Dear Sir:—We ask for a Divine warrant, a "thus saith the Lord," either expressed or implied, by which the exclusive doctrine can be sustained. And here we feel it to be a privilege to say that with such writers as the late Dr. M'Master, the controversy is greatly narrowed. He candidly acknowledges "that the use of a faithful version of such songs as Isaiah 26 : 1–9 and Revelation 5 : 9–13 would *not corrupt* the worship of God."* Very different is the doctrine held by the authors quoted at the beginning of the last Letter.

Admitting for argument's sake, that in "Rouse's paraphrase" they sing "the Psalms which God has given," without admixture of "human composition," and without omission or error—the question now is, "where is the Scriptural *authority* for restricting the church under her present dispensation to the book of Psalms?"

The nearest approach to such a Divine appointment, so far as we have observed, is found in 2 Chronicles 29 : 30. "Hezekiah the king and the princes commanded the Levites to sing praise unto the Lord with the words of David, and of Asaph the seer."† This occurred in the great reformation under that pious sovereign. It clearly establishes a Divine warrant to sing the sacred songs composed by David and Asaph in the temple service, and by the Jewish church. But this direction to the Levites

* Apology, p. 96.

† This passage is often quoted in proof by these brethren.

does not prove the positions assumed by these brethren for several reasons:

1. It proves *too much*, because it equally establishes instrumental music in the church of the present period. In verse 25 we read: "Hezekiah set the Levites in the house of the Lord with cymbals, with psalteries, and with harps, *according to the commandment of David*, and of Gad the king's seer, and of Nathan the prophet." Here, in the same connection, are directions equally explicit for the use of choirs and various instruments in praising God! It is obvious, therefore, that every inspired direction for the temple service is *not* necessarily a command binding upon the church of the new dispensation. Nor was this appointment of a magnificent choir of several thousand persons and numerous musical instruments, a mere temporary arrangement for that special reformation. We find that two hundred years later, at the foundation of the second temple under Ezra, and in the days of the prophets Haggai and Zechariah, "they set the priests with trumpets, and the Levites the sons of Asaph with cymbals, to praise the Lord, after the *ordinance of David king of Israel*."* The obligation from such texts as these, to sing exclusively with David and Asaph their literal Psalms, is no more express than to copy their choir and introduce their trumpets, cymbals, &c. And to make this reasoning still more conclusive, in 2 Chronicles 7 : 6, these harps, trumpets, cymbals, &c., are called, "*instruments of music of the Lord*, which David the king had made to praise the Lord!" "INSTRUMENTS OF MUSIC OF THE LORD!" The United Presbyterian "Testimony" argues that because the Psalms are called "*songs of the Lord*," they must be of perpetual obligation in praise, just as we read of "the table of the Lord," "the day of the Lord," which are said to imply *Divine authority* and appointment.† But the argument

* Ezra 3 : 10.

† Testimony, p. 44. In 1 Chronicles 16 : 42, these trumpets, cymbals, harps, &c., are called "musical instruments of God." Of course they are of perpetual appointment in Divine worship!

is quite as strong from the phrase, "instruments of the Lord," to prove the perpetual obligation of harps, trumpets, &c. Thus we arrive, with the friends of the "Testimony," at this conclusion, viz. "that these directions and examples are *still in force*, as there is no New Testament intimation to the contrary."* If Christ and his apostles ever revoked this appointment of "the instruments of the Lord," let it be shown. And to render the difficulty still more embarrassing, one of the favorite proof texts quoted in the "Testimony" is Psalm 81 : 2, which while it enjoins to "take a Psalm," immediately adds: "Bring hither the timbrel, the pleasant harp with the psaltery!" Nor need we inform these testifying brethren where to find such inspired directions as these: "Praise the Lord with the sound of a trumpet; praise him with with the psaltery and harp; praise him with the timbrel and dance; praise him with stringed instruments and organs." Psalm 150. If "the Psalm" is made perpetual and exclusive by the "ordinance of David," why not "the instruments of the Lord" made perpetual by the same "ordinance?" The argument from 2 Chronicles 29 : 30, thus proves too much, and therefore proves nothing to the point. We are far from desiring to exclude the book of Psalms from the devotions of the church. But the acts of Hezekiah are not the proofs on which we rely to designate the proper position of that inspired and very precious book in the worship of God. But we shall speak of this more fully in a future Letter.

2. The argument from 2 Chronicles 29 : 30 in favor of the doctrine of our brethren, fails in another point of view. Thirteen years later, Hezekiah himself composed a Psalm for the "house of the Lord," and gave directions that his "songs" should be sung in the temple service all the days of his life. This was shown in our last Letter. How then could that pious prince have viewed "the words of David and Asaph" as the exclusive Psalmody of the church? He evidently did not so un-

* Testimony, p. 44.

derstand his own *command* as recorded 2 Chronicles 29 : 30. Of the one hundred and fifty pieces which are said to have constituted the Psalmody of the Jewish church, David wrote a little over *seventy*, and Asaph not over *twelve*, probably only ten. The others are variously ascribed to Heman, Jeduthun, Solomon, Moses and other authors. It is with surprise, therefore, we find in the United Presbyterian "Testimony" the following in relation to the book of Psalms: "The title given to David *their penman*, ('sweet Psalmist of Israel,') indicates that they should be used," &c. Why David was the *penman* of not more *than half* of those sacred songs! Quite a number of them are referred, by the most eminent authorities, to periods long after David was in his grave; and some of these songs to the times during and subsequent to the seventy years' captivity! How, then, could Hezekiah regard "the words of David and Asaph" as the exclusive Psalmody of the church? Even if "David and Asaph" were the authors of the whole "book of Psalms," Hezekiah's example is *against*, rather than in favor of the exclusive doctrine.

3. We object to *the argument* derived from 2 Chronicles 29 : 30, because it is inconsistent with 2 Chronicles 35 : 25—"And Jeremiah lamented for Josiah; and all the singing-men and the singing-women spake of Josiah in their lamentations *to this day*, and made them AN ORDINANCE IN ISRAEL: and, behold, they are written in the Lamentations." We regard this passage as quite as good authority for singing the book of "Lamentations" in Divine worship as the acts of Hezekiah for the *perpetual and exclusive use* of "the words of David and Asaph!" Yet this "ordinance in Israel" (or the church) was made under the eye and approval of Jeremiah, more than one hundred years after the acts of Hezekiah in 2 Chronicles 29. So evident is it that the church of that period did not receive "the words of David and Asaph" as her exclusive Psalmody.

For such reasons as these we are constrained to regard

these acts of Hezekiah as no *Divine warrant* for the "book of Psalms" as *the system* of praise to be used in the church of our day; much less as of *exclusive* authority for that purpose.

But it is further argued that "the peculiar character of their matter * * * indicates the *particular end* for which these sacred songs were intended."* Now we cordially admit that in this book the "glory of Jehovah is celebrated in the sublimest strains of Eastern poetry," &c. But is there no such *suitable matter* in the other parts of the Scriptures? Are all the "Psalms, hymns and spiritual songs" composed by Isaiah, Jeremiah, and the others, and in the whole of the New Testament, "*unfit to be sung?*" Was not much of this *suitable matter* composed in the form of Psalms and hymns and used by inspired men, who also *commanded the church* "to sing these *new songs?*" For proof of these points see our previous Letter.

But whilst every pious heart will cordially respond to much that is said in praise of the book of Psalms, nothing is easier than to prove that *large portions* of many of these songs are quite as prosaic as the historical parts of Isaiah and the other prophets, and in that view, at least, quite as "unfit to be sung." For example, see parts of Psalms 78, 105, 106, &c. What more *unlike* "the sublimest strains of Eastern poetry" than the following specimens:

He brought among them swarms of flies,
Which did them sore annoy:
And divers kinds of filthy frogs
He sent them to destroy.

His word all sorts of *flies and lice*
In all their borders brings.

Do to them as to Midian;
Jabin and Kison strand;
And Sisra, which at Endor fell
As dung to fat the land.

* Pressly on Psalmody, p. 72.

My wounds do stink and are corrupt;
My folly makes it so.

Moab s my washing pot; my shoe
I'll over Edom throw.

Whose belly with thy treasure hid
Thou fill'st—they children have
In plenty. Of their goods the rest
They to their children leave.

It was no doubt in view of such stanzas as the foregoing, that Prof. Beveridge, of Xenia, wrote as follows: "A few expressions are employed which can scarcely be considered as suitable in dignity either to *the ordinance* or THE MATTER of praise; such as 'I'm like a broken pot,' 'as fat as grease they be,' 'which admiration breed,' 'the hairy scalp,' &c. This language Dr. Beveridge reported and published as the chairman of a committee of the Associate Synod."*

It would be easy to collect many parallel specimens. We are not now complaining of *the verse* of Rouse, which some have called "discord and jargon." Neither have we the slightest objection to these and hundreds of similar passages as they stand in *God's inspired word.* The *only* question now before us relates to the most "suitable matter" for praise. And in view of such passages it is obvious that we cannot speak of many parts of these Divine songs in such terms as sublime strains of Eastern poetry. The preacher rises in the sacred desk, and commences to read:

I like an owl in desert am,
That nightly there doth moan.

When they me saw, they from me fled,
Ev'n so I am forgot.
As men are out of mind when dead;
I'm like a broken pot.

That in the blood of enemies
Thy foot imbrued may be;
And of thy dogs dipped in the same
The tongues thou mayest see.

* Evangelical Repository, April, 1851.

The spearman's host, the multitude
Of bulls which fiercely look,
Those calves which people forth have sent,
O Lord our God rebuke.

These can scarcely be called sublime strains of poetry. Whatever may have been the poetical forms of the Hebrew (which are now lost) we have no "Divine warrant," under any pretext, to speak of these and similar passages, as any other than they really are. They were composed for a people and for times of great simplicity of manners. But in the progress of refinement under the gospel, it is no more *a reproach* to the Psalms to say that such passages are not *as suitable* for public song as many parts of the other Scriptures, than it is a reproach to the Holy Spirit to say that Deut. 23 : 1, though read publicly to the Jews, is not the most suitable part of "all Scripture which is profitable for *instruction*," to be read from the pulpit! Nothing would be easier than to name other texts which these brethren themselves *studiously avoid*, though "given by inspiration"—and thus they are guilty *of the very sin* which they charge upon Dr. Watts, viz. "laying aside *as useless* parts of God's word!" * They *lay aside* from *being publicly read*—we *lay aside* from purposes of praise. Which is the greater crime, good sense can determine.

But we are also referred to "*the titles* which the Holy Spirit has employed to designate these Divine hymns," and which, we are told, "indicate the *particular use* for which they were intended." "The Holy Spirit appropriates to this collection of sacred songs the title, 'the book of Psalms,' and by this title they are repeatedly referred to in the New Testament." "The word 'Psalm' is of Greek derivation, and comes from a word which signifies to sing. Psalms, then, are songs which are to be sung." †

It is not denied, that for the most part, the Psalms were given to the Jews to be used in their worship, and

* Pressly on Psalmody, p. 112.
† Pressly, p. 73.

were therefore called Tehillim, Praises. But does it necessarily follow, that as a system of Psalmody they are divinely required to be sung under the present dispensation, in every thought, sentiment and expression? No more than "all Scripture given by inspiration of God" is binding *to be read* in public worship. Besides, these brethren themselves "lay aside as useless" the 20th verse of the 72d Psalm, most of the inspired titles, &c., as already shown. Again, if the general title of the book is of any avail in this argument, we must go to the original Hebrew. There we find that instead of being called "book of Psalms," the title is "book of Praises." *Tehillim*, the Hebrew plural of *Tehillah*, is not the word usually rendered *Psalms*. It is the separate title of but one Psalm (145th) in the whole book, and that in the singular. So far as we have observed, it is never in any other connection, translated by the Septuagint *Psalmos*, Psalm, but generally by a word meaning praise, or praises. *Sepher Tehillim*, or rather "Tehillim," is the Hebrew title, and the exact rendering is "book of Praises," * not "book of Psalms."

We admit that the title *Biblos Psalmon*, "book of Psalms," in the Septuagint or Greek translation is cited in the New Testament. But we shall show presently that this fact does not necessarily give it Divine sanction. And the propriety of some more general title, such as "book of Praises," is obvious; because several of these songs have the title "a Prayer;" such as the 17th, "Prayer of David," the 90th, "Prayer of Moses," &c. To show the exceedingly various character of these compositions, learned men have classified them as follows: "*Sixty-six* are prayers, twenty-nine are songs of thanksgiving, thirty are Psalms of praise and adoration, forty are on general topics of instruction, ten are prophetical, and three are historical."† Such is the various character of these "*Praises.*"

* Horne's Introduction, vol. 4, p. 115.

† Dr. Scott says, "The Hebrew name of this book is *Tehillim* or *Praises*."

Thus it seems that of this collection of Prayers, Praises, Prophecies, History, Doctrine, &c., the only original and inspired title, is "book of Praises." But are there no *praises* without *Psalms and singing?* What says the book itself? "Praise God with the sound of the trumpet; praise him with the timbrel and *dance*," &c. Psalm 150. "And David *danced* before the Lord with all his might." 2 Samuel 6 : 14. Besides, is there no acceptable *praise* in *prayer*, which forms so large a proportion of the book? We do not commonly *sing* our prayers, though two of the constituent elements of prayer are "adoration and thanksgiving." So our Catechism teaches us in the "conclusion of the Lord's prayer," "that in our prayers we *praise* Him;" and the same is true when the Psalms are read from the pulpit and in family worship.

The general title, "book of Praises," does obviously include all these methods of praising God, and therefore contains no infallible indication of the *particular use* for which the Psalms were intended, especially no "Divine warrant" for their exclusive use in singing praise.

But we are told that the Holy Spirit by quoting in the New Testament the Septuagint translation of the original title *(Biblos Psalmon)*, "appropriates to this collection of songs the title "book of Psalms." * We concede that it is so quoted, but we deny the inference. All sound Biblical critics admit that the translation of the Old Testament in the Greek Septuagint is very often *grossly erroneous*. It is also a settled point that "the inspired writers of the New Testament often make citations from the Septuagint, even when *notoriously in error, provided* the blunders were of such a nature as not to *weaken the special proofs* for which the citations were made." † It would be easy to fill pages with quotations to establish these points.

* Pressly on Psalmody, p. 73.

† Horne's Introduction, vol. 2, p. 386. Horne adds, "The Psalms and the Prophets were translated by men *every way unequal* to the task." He means in the Septuagint.

What, then, was the case under consideration? The inspired writers of the New Testament using the Greek language, merely wished to refer to the "book of Praises" by its general title. The *error* of the Septuagint in calling it "book of Psalms," could not in the least weaken the reference, or in any way affect it. According to their usual custom, therefore, they quoted it as they found it, sufficiently correct for their purpose. But the *mere fact* of quotation in this case, no more proves that the Holy Spirit *appropriates* the Septuagint title, and thereby gives it Divine sanction, than scores of similar citations by New Testament writers prove that the Holy Spirit *approves* the grossest blunders in the learned languages, and in fact adopts *sheer nonsense.*

Nor is it of any weight in this discussion, that "the word *Psalm* is of Greek derivation, and signifies to sing." The truth is, that while in the New Testament it is sometimes thus used, the original primary meaning conveys the idea *of playing on an instrument.* This, too, is the original meaning of the Hebrew verb *zamar* (from which comes *mizmor*, a *Psalm*), viz. "to *touch*, or *strike* the chords of an instrument, to *play*, Greek *psallein;* and hence to *sing*, to *chant*, as *accompanying an instrument.*"*

The title "Psalm," therefore, proves too much for these brethren. As derived from the Old Testament worship it would sanction in our churches the use of instrumental music, for such is the uniform history of Psalmody under the ancient dispensation, especially in the public service of the church. The use of the title "Psalm," no more proves that all the Psalms are now *to be sung* literally in every sentiment and expression, than it proves that all are to be accompanied with stringed instruments, organs, harps, cymbals, trumpets, &c., especially since the Psalmist himself equally exhorts to the use of all these methods of praise, Psalm 150; and Hezekiah's precept and example include the use of these "instruments of God."

* Gesenius, Hebrew Lex., *in verbo.*

From these considerations we trust it will be evident how feeble is the argument from the original "titles" of the book of Psalms. And to give additional force to our reasoning, let it be observed that in Hebrew, one of the specific titles often used for particular Psalms, is *Shir*, a song. It is found some thirty times, and in the original seems to refer *to the use of the voice.* Hence we read of "the daughters of song," and it is employed to denote the act of singing, as in 2 Chronicles 23 : 18. Now if the general title, "book of Psalms," proves that they were "intended to be sung," then by the same reasoning the general title, *Shir Hashirim*, "the song of songs," proves that "Solomon's Song" is in all ages *to be sung* in public worship! This result, we think, is legitimately reached by the logic of our brethren themselves. Here is an inspired *song* with one of the titles of the Psalms—more than this, it is "the song of songs," "the most excellent of songs!" It is pronounced by its author *superior* to all the PSALMS which bear the same title, for it is "most excellent!" Surely then it is, it *must* be "intended to be sung in the worship of God." In addition, "this is most evident from the peculiar character of *its matter.*" * Dr. Scott, that eminently pious and judicious commentator, well remarks, "NO OTHER POEM IN THE WORLD so well describes the state of the believer's heart, and is so adapted to excite *admiring*. *adoring, grateful love* to God our Saviour, as this." The subjects of the whole book are Christ and his church, and well does it deserve the inspired title, "song of songs," or "the most excellent of songs." Why, then, we repeat, if the title-logic is worth anything, is it excluded from the Psalmody of these brethren?

And to enforce this conclusion, hear the celebrated Ralph Erskine, one of the original fathers and founders of the Associate or Seceder Presbytery in Scotland—"When the motion was made of turning *all the Scripture songs* into common metre, FOR THE SAME USE WITH

* See Pressly on Psalmody, p. 73.

THE PSALMS OF DAVID, I was also urged to make a version of this song, &c."* Again he says, "This sacred book of Scripture (the Song of Solomon) contains the *sweetest* and *noblest* instances of the grace of Christ toward his church and people." And in stating and defending the nature of his previous paraphrase, he adds, "If more seem to be said upon any verse *than is directly imported in it*, I hope it will be reckoned no great fault, if what is said be deducible from it, or necessary for the further *explication* of it, and for *adapting* this *paraphrase upon an Old Testament song to a New Testament dispensation*."† So obvious is it, that Ralph Erskine and his compeers never *dreamed* of "*a Divine appointment* of a fair and literal version" of the Psalms as of exclusive authority for all ages. In regard to these topics, Erskine held the principles of the Presbyterian church—and the views of his modern successors are recent "human discoveries." Thus evident is it that the Associate church of this country have turned aside from the good "old paths" in which their fathers walked, in the purest and best days of Reformation!

But perhaps some one may reply that "the Song of Solomon" was never employed, so far as we know, in the temple worship. Very true, and therefore the proof is complete that the use of the title *Shir*, a song, though employed to designate about thirty of the Psalms, settles nothing in favor of their perpetual use as the matter of praise; since the *superlative* form of the same title did not prove "the song of songs" to be the matter of praise, not even to the Jews. Of course Dr. Pressly's title argument falls to the ground.

* He elsewhere says—"The first public recommendation was by the Associate Synod, anno 1747." Works, vol. 10, p. 425.

† Works, vol. 10, p. 316.

LETTER VIII.

DISCUSSION CONTINUED — "DIVINE WARRANT" IN PAUL'S "PSALMS, HYMNS AND SPIRITUAL SONGS" — EXAMINATION OF THE SEPTUAGINT USE OF THESE TITLES — THE FACT THAT THE PSALMS WERE ORIGINALLY GIVEN TO BE SUNG, DOES NOT PROVE THEM TO BE A PERPETUAL AND UNCHANGEABLE SYSTEM OF PRAISE — VARIOUS UNSOUND ARGUMENTS EXPOSED.

MY DEAR SIR:—In my last I commenced the inquiry: Where do our brethren discover "a Divine warrant" for restricting the praises of the church under her present dispensation, to the book of Psalms? Such a *warrant* is not found in the acts of Hezekiah (2 Chronicles 29 : 30), nor yet in the general title of the book itself, as we trust we have proved. It is granted, for the present argument, that they employ in their worship "the very Psalms which God has given," "the Psalms of inspiration," "the songs composed in heaven," (all which we utterly deny and have shown to be far otherwise.) But conceding this, the inquiry returns: Where is the "thus saith the Lord," which hath established in his church this one book of songs as her only, all-sufficient and perpetual Psalm book to the end of time? This is now the question—and we proceed to examine a third argument on which our brethren seem greatly to rely. It assumes the form of an express command of the New Testament.

In Colossians 3 : 16, Paul exhorts the church as follows: "Let the word of Christ dwell in you richly in all wisdom; teaching and admonishing one another, in psalms, and hymns and spiritual songs, singing with grace in your hearts to the Lord." (A parallel passage, is Ephesians 5 : 19.) It is true, indeed, that these texts have always been viewed as strongholds of the Presbyterian doctrine, viz. that it is the duty and privilege of the church to praise God not only with *Psalms*, but with any other "hymns and songs" found in the inspired writings. But our brethren have endeavored to turn this old Presbyterian battery against us in the following method, which we will state as briefly as possible: "When Paul was addressing the Colossians," they argue, "he wrote in the Greek language, and the translation of the Old Testament then used generally in the Christian church was the Greek Septuagint. Hence when Paul enjoined the use of 'Psalms, hymns and spiritual songs,' he merely quoted in Greek the Septuagint translation of several of the Hebrew titles of the Psalms, i. e., he wrote the Greek *Psalmois*, *humnois*, *odais*, instead of the Hebrew titles *Mizmorim*, *Tehillim*, *Shirim*, both sets of terms meaning Psalms, hymns and songs." Hence, they argue, Paul's injunction to sing "Psalms, hymns and spiritual songs," is equivalent to a command to sing the various Psalms of David which in Paul's Greek Bible bore these titles, being correct translations of the three Hebrew titles, *Mizmorim*, *Tehillim*, *Shirim*.*

But this argument fails to produce conviction for several reasons:

1. It is an error to assert, as these brethren do, that the three Hebrew titles, *Mizmorim*, *Tehillim*, *Shirim*, "are *particularly used* to designate these different compositions," viz. "the sacred poems of the book of Psalms."† *Tehillah*, (the singular of *Tehillim*,) which they say means *hymn*, (Greek, *humnos*,) is the title of *only one* Psalm (145th), and is not rendered by the Septuagint *humnos*, but *ainesis*, that is, *praise*. Our English Bibles supply the word Psalm, and read it "Psalm of *praise*." The plural *Tehillim*, is never used for a title of a particular Psalm, but only as the general title of the whole book; and the Septuagint translates it not *humnoi*, hymns, but *psalmoi*, Psalms. This spoils the whole ar-

* Pressly on Psalmody, (abridged) p. 39; Testimony of United Presbyterian church, p. 45.

† Pressly on Psalmody.

gument. If Paul used the Septuagint translation, he could not possibly have meant the term *humnoi*, hymns, to be a translation of *Tehillim*, because the Septuagint do not so translate *Tehillim;* they translate it *psalmoi*, Psalms. It follows, therefore, that if the apostle intended to cite the Hebrew terms as rendered into Greek by the Septuagint, he must have exhorted the Colossians to sing "*Psalms, and Psalms* and spiritual songs"—for the Septuagint translation of both *Mizmorim* and *Tehillim* is *Psalms.*

Again: So far is it from being correct to say that "the Hebrew terms for Psalms, hymns and songs are *particularly* used to designate the different compositions" of the book of Psalms, that there are five or six of these titles besides the three mentioned, all but one of which are used *more particularly* than *Tehillah*, one of them as much as twelve times. It is incorrect, therefore, to assert that these three terms are *particularly* used.

2. The term *humnos*, hymn, is never used by the Septuagint as a distinctive title of any Psalm. We read in the titles very often *Psalm*, Psalm of David, but never *humnos*, hymn of David.* It is not denied that the dative plural, *humnois*, is found in the title of Psalm 67, and others—but what does it mean? Does it mean *hymns?* Read the title of Psalm 67: "To the chief musician on *neginoth*, a Psalm of David." Here the Septuagint translate *neginoth* by *humnois, hymns!* And what is the meaning of *neginoth?* It signifies "stringed instruments to be played on by the fingers." This is the sort of *hymns* meant by the Septuagint. But worse still—in Psalm 4, the same Septuagint translate *neginoth* by *psalmois*, Psalms! So that these ancient Jewish musical instruments signify both *Psalms* and *hymns!* Thus according to the Septuagint logic, Paul must have exhorted the Colossians, (1) to teach and admonish one

* In Psalm 72 : 20, the Septuagint use *humnoi* to express what our Bibles call "the *prayers* of David"—but the Hebrew is not *Tehillim*, but another word meaning properly "prayers," not *hymns*. This is not even a seeming exception to our statement.

another with *Psalms*, i. e., with *neginoth*, or "stringed instruments;" (2) with *neginoth* again, i. e., with "stringed instruments," or *hymns;* and (3) with spiritual songs. And our brethren would persuade us that the apostle quoted these absurd Greek titles from the Septuagint, and gave them his inspired sanction !* Well might the very learned Horne pronounce the Septuagint translation of the Psalms to be worthless for purposes of criticism.

3. As to the third of the titles supposed to have been cited by the apostle, viz. *odais pneumatikois*, "spiritual songs," it is sufficient to say that there is no such title in the Septuagint—of course Paul could not have quoted it. The term *ode*, a song, is one of the Septuagint titles, but that is not the same thing with "spiritual songs."

But granting for the present, that when the apostle exhorted to the use of "Psalms, hymns and spiritual songs," he intended to quote the *psalmoi, humnoi, odai* of the Septuagint—what does it prove? Certainly not that he had *exclusive* reference to these titles in the book of Psalms. The two last terms, *humnos* and *ode*, are used by the Septuagint to designate other portions of the inspired writings; and why may not Paul have referred to those other "hymns and songs" not embraced in the book of Psalms? Thus in Isaiah 42 : 10: "Sing unto the Lord *a new song*," (Septuagint, *humnon.*) Why may not Paul have had in his eye the sublime and beautiful address of Moses (Deuteronomy 32), delivered just before his death, and in the previous chapter called *ode* by the Septuagint, not less than three times? Thus chapter 31 : 19: "Now therefore write ye this *song*," &c. Why may not the apostle have had his eye upon such *humnoi* and *odai*, "hymns and songs" as these, as they are found outside of the book of Psalms? If he had reference to such as these, then what becomes of the argument of these brethren? Paul's exhortation to sing "hymns and spiritual songs" becomes an inspired au-

* "The Psalms (of the Septuagint) were translated by men every way unequal to the task."—*Horne's Introduction*, vol. 2, p. 168.

thority for the Presbyterian doctrine of Psalmody. Nor can we doubt for a moment, that *ours* is the correct interpretation, since it alone shields the apostle from a needless tautology or repetition, as though he designed to exhort the Colossians to sing "*Psalms, Psalms and Psalms!*" Indeed, it is not denied that the interpretation we oppose *does* involve this tautology. "These different terms, 'Psalms, hymns and spiritual songs,'" "probably indicate sacred songs which are substantially the same;" "they are substantially of the same import."* In view of all these considerations, it is plain that this argument from the Septuagint titles is an utter failure.

The argument from "the peculiar matter," and from "the titles" of the Psalms, having been reviewed, we proceed to a third point:

(iii.) "From the fact that God has given to his church a book of Psalms, it would appear to be the Divine will that this should be used to the exclusion of all others."†

From the first part of this statement, no Presbyterian will dissent. We cordially maintain that the Psalms, which were gradually composed, were given to the Jews, the ancient visible church, by their glorious Author, as a very precious portion of the inspired records.‡ Nor can it be denied that many of these sacred songs were sung in the temple service by a magnificent choir of several thousand Levites, accompanied with matchless strains of instrumental music—such, probably, as the world never heard before or since. The composition of these songs having been completed, about three hundred years after the period of Hezekiah they were collected into a book, as a part of the sacred canon. But we have no reason to believe that the church, either then or for centuries previous, was restricted to the precise songs now contained in the book of Psalms. On the contrary, the example

* Pressly on Psalmody, p. 141.

† Pressly, p. 87.

‡ Their composition extended through many centuries, and they were collected and arranged by Ezra, as is supposed.

of Hezekiah in preparing and ordering the singing of a song or songs, and of Jeremiah in sanctioning the singing of the Lamentations for Josiah, proves the very reverse. And when it is inferred from such premises, that the same exact system of songs, so many, no more and no less, must necessarily be the Psalmody of the Christian dispensation to the end of the world—there is a gap in the logic. There is no positive proof, not even strong presumptive evidence, which will justify such a conclusion. For much proof to the contrary, see our Letter VI.

With the statements already made before our minds, we open the New Testament. Do we there discover no forms of public and private praise, except in the words of the book of Psalms? Far otherwise. The writers of the New Testament quote these sacred songs not less than *sixty* times, but *never* in any instance do they cite a *complete song* of praise; only in three or four instances do they introduce a *brief extract* as a part of their expressions of praise, and in every such case they amend by additions of their own. Nor do they ever speak of the book as a system of Psalmody. The apostles and our Lord often mention the Psalms, the book of Psalms and David, without quoting them, but they are commonly referred to precisely like any other portions of the Old Testament Scriptures, as they doubtless would have referred to "the Song of songs," but not associated with singing at all. Thus when citing the 22d Psalm, on the subject of the crucifixion, the evangelist says: "That it might be fulfilled which was spoken by the prophet, They parted my garments, and for my vesture they cast lots." See for similar examples, Matthew 13 : 35, 26 : 35; Luke 2 : 42, 24 : 44. In truth, if the Psalms had never been sung at all, the New Testament, in such quotations as these, could not have observed a more profound silence on the subject of their "particular designation." James indeed exhorts: "Is any merry, let him sing Psalms." But the word "Psalms" is not in the original — it is simply "let him sing," *psalleto*. Nor if he had used the express term *psalmous*, would it have necessarily confined his meaning to the book of Psalms. The term has a much wider meaning.

The same result is reached when we observe in what sort of song the New Testament saints were accustomed to express their fervent thanksgivings to their Creator and Redeemer. How did Mary and Zacharias and Elizabeth praise God? By repeating one of the Old Testament Psalms? No such thing. Read the record in Luke 1. What sort of a song was that which John heard sung in the presence of "Him that sitteth on the throne?" Was it one of the Psalms of David? Listen—"Thou art worthy to take the book, * * * for thou wast slain and hast redeemed us to God by thy blood. * * * Worthy is the Lamb that was slain to receive power and riches and wisdom and glory and blessing." And the apostle himself, when about to commence his record of the wonderful mysteries of the closing book of inspiration, as though he could not restrain his emotions, breaks forth, "Unto him that loved us and washed us from our sins in his own blood," &c. These are merely specimens of the Psalmody which meets our eye the instant we open the New Testament. What person, having respect for the example of primitive Christianity, can have any doubt as to the duty and privilege of singing such songs as these.*

There is, as it seems to us, a vast amount of loose logic current on these topics. Thus, "If the songs contained

* In the preface to Ralph Erskine's "Scripture Songs from the four Evangelists," published at Falkirk, Scotland, 1796, the editor says: "Many parts of it (the Psalms of David) are peculiarly adapted to the Old Testament dispensation of carnal rites and ceremonies, * * * and not so perspicuously clear and full of the grace and spirit of the Gospel," viz. as the New Testament. "This," he adds, "has induced many devout and piously disposed persons ardently and sincerely to wish that our *Psalmody* were enlarged * * * by selections out of the Old Testament, and a number from the New." "The latter," he says, "yields so much agreeable matter of *praise*, and very suitable matter of songs and Divine hymns." Works, vol. 10, p. 627.

in the book of Psalms were given to the church to be used in the praises of God, it will then be admitted that the point in dispute is settled." * What point is settled? No one denies that the Psalms were given to the ancient Jewish church, and for the most part to be sung; but does that *settle* the further question, "Do these one hundred and fifty Psalms compose the exclusive Psalmody of the church under her new dispensation?" Take a parallel specimen of reasoning—The written revelation of God to the ancient church, consisted of "the Law, the Prophets and the Psalms." God was to be worshiped by the public reading of these Scriptures—they were given for this purpose. What point does this settle? Not surely that all other portions of Divine revelation in the New Testament must be excluded from the public reading in the house of God.

Here is another example of bad logic. "The book of Psalms, whence was it? From heaven or of men? If from heaven, why not use it?"† We reply—"The Law and the Prophets, whence were they?" "If from heaven, why not use them" to the exclusion of the New Testament Scriptures? The heavenly origin of the book of Psalms no one doubts, and we rejoice "*to use it*" for every purpose for which it was designed under the new dispensation. But that it was intended to be an exclusive system of Psalmody to all ages, is *the very point* to be proved. Of course the argument from its Divine origin is a mere begging of the question. "The Song of Solomon," and all the other songs and hymns scattered throughout the pages of the Bible, are *all "from heaven."* Does it follow that they are all to be used in public praise? If our brethren will follow their own reasoning to this result, it will narrow the discussion to a very small point.

Another specimen. "When we consider how frequently the apostles introduce the Psalms in their dis-

* Pressly on Psalmody, p. 70.

† Testimony of the United Presbyterian church, p. 44.

courses and epistles, *we cannot doubt* that they regarded the matter of these sacred songs as very suitable to be employed in the worship of God." * But the fact is that the prophecies of Isaiah are *more frequently* quoted in the New Testament than the Psalms. Of course it follows that "*they are even more suitable*" for public praise! Similar errors in reasoning are very frequent in connection with the inspiration of the Psalms, and it is boldly affirmed that "no argument is needed to prove that Rouse's version *is the word of God!*" † But if this were even so, are not the Law and the Prophets "the word of God?" But this does not prove that they are to be *read* from the pulpit, to the exclusion of the whole New Testament! To allege the "Divine appointment" of the Psalms to be sung to solve the difficulty, is a sheer *petitio principii*—a begging of the question.

Much importance in the argument, seems to be attached to the circumstance, that the Psalms have been collected into a separate "book" in the great volume of inspiration, and the inference is thence deduced that the object was to furnish an all-sufficient system of Psalmody for the church in all future ages. But here again the premises are too narrow to support the conclusion. On the supposition that these inspired compositions were to be preserved for the spiritual benefit of the church, and to be used in other modes besides song, how natural and reasonable that they should be grouped together and hold a separate place among the varied productions of the Holy Spirit? This was precisely what every intelligent mind would anticipate, viz. that these sacred odes should be embodied in a single book. The probable reason why a very few are found, not literally but *substantially* in other parts of the Bible, was that this was necessary for the integrity and completeness of the historical narrative, as in 2 Chronicles, chapter 22, compared with Psalm 18—though in this and other

* Pressly on Psalmody, p. 91.
† Dodd's Reply, p. 89.

cases there are very numerous points of difference. How would any intelligent uninspired editor act under similar circumstances? If called to arrange and publish the works of a deceased friend, would not this grouping together of the different species of composition be a first dictate of common sense? It would be utterly absurd if such editor, in issuing the works of Cowper, for example, should throw together in promiscuous mass his fugitive poems and his familiar letters!

Again—If, as these brethren maintain, the songs of the church are to be restricted to one small portion of the inspired records, and if in disregarding this Divine limitation so far as to sing parts of Isaiah or the New Testament, we only expose ourselves to the Divine displeasure, instead of having our sacrifices accepted—then certainly we are entitled to know very accurately, the time, place, personal agency, and other circumstances attending this "appointment" of an exclusive Psalmody for all coming ages.

We are not inquiring as to the authority of the "book of Psalms" as an integral part of Holy Writ, given "for our learning." This is just as plain in relation to that book as to Isaiah and the other inspired writings. Neither is it a question merely of arrangement and classification "for doctrine, reproof, instruction," &c. There is no difficulty in such points as these. But we think we are entitled to particular information as to *the person* by whom *the number* of the Psalms was fixed at precisely one hundred and fifty, neither more nor less, for *the express purpose* of Psalmody to the exclusion of all other songs, inspired and uninspired. How and when was he appointed by the Great Author of Inspiration to establish this Divine "ordinance" and place a *limit* around it like to that which encircled Mount Sinai, with the terrible inscription, "*Pass not over* LEST THOU DIE!" We have a *right* to demand of these brethren a clear "thus saith the Lord" on these topics.

That we are entitled to demand full satisfaction on

these subjects, is obvious from the reasoning of these brethren themselves. When pressing their point in argument, they are accustomed to remind us in the most solemn manner, of "the terrible death of Nadab and Abihu;" and that "we have reason to apprehend that the disregard of Divine *authority* in the worship of God, will now subject *the guilty* to the displeasure of heaven *as certainly*," &c. And they further allege that when *they* happen to meet with Presbyterian congregations, "*they are compelled to remain silent*, lest they should be chargeable with offering *strange fire* before the Lord." * And citing the Jewish law in regard to bloody sacrifices, they point us to the certain destruction which awaited the presumptuous worshiper who should dare to present to the Lord "the flesh of the pig" instead of that of "the kid." † But as if all this were not enough, we are charged with taking "impious license" with the book of Psalms, and the whole is enforced by the awful malediction: "Add thou not unto his words, lest he reprove thee and thou be found a liar." ‡

But if all this be intended for anything more than rhetorical flourish, it must be obvious that we are entitled to require "the *pattern* showed in the mount." The most minute and express directions were divinely given to Moses and Aaron in relation to the Levitical offerings, and in the erection of the altar of sacrifices nothing could be more explicit than that it was to be made "of earth," not of "hewn stone," and that "no tool was to be lifted up upon it." Exodus 20 : 24, 25. If these brethren really believe that Presbyterians are exposed to such judgments as those of Nadab and Abihu—if the crime is so flagrant and the penalty so certain, as they pretend, let them produce the Divine "pattern." We demand the express directions of the Holy Spirit, or at least fair inferential proof, setting the fearful *limit* around the book

* Pressly on Psalmody, pp. 9, 10.
† Pressly on Psalmody.
‡ Apology, p. 114.

of Psalms. But if no such directions are to be found, then we would warn these brethren of the folly and criminality of attempting to call "down fire from heaven" upon all who "do not follow with them."

It is no sufficient answer to the foregoing reasoning, to allege that the canon of Scripture was arranged by Ezra, and the Psalms were placed in their present position by an inspired hand. That is not the point. The canon would have been equally authoritative and complete, if there had been no "book of Psalms," i. e., if these sacred songs had been inserted in the lives of David and the other penmen of the Holy Spirit. The question is, "among all the variety of devotional poetry in the Bible, *what Divine oracle* has selected and fixed by a perpetual decree, or at least by fair inference, an inspired psalter of one hundred and fifty songs as the *only* and *all-sufficient* volume of praise to all ages?" If no answer can be given to this inquiry, then "where there is no law, there is no transgression;" and we treat with derision pages of vapid denunciation as the empty flourish of feeble rhetoric. And we are the rather encouraged to this, because the self-same logic which hurls upon our heads the penalties of the Jewish theocracy, would lead to the stoning of a man to death for "gathering sticks on the Sabbath." Numbers 15 : 32.

But it is said with much confidence, that "there is no book of Psalms in the New Testament. Nor is there any promise of the influences of the Holy Spirit to assist any man in preparing one." * How is this to be accounted for? We reply — no inspired *book* of Psalms for the new dispensation was necessary. The theory of the Presbyterian church is complete and satisfactory without any New Testament volume of praise. We find a rich and varied supply both in the Old Testament and in the New; in the former, especially in the book of Psalms—in the latter, not only all the noble songs and hymns sung by angels at the birth of Christ, &c., by the glorified church

* Pressly on Psalmody, p. 85.

and by inspired men, but besides, hundreds of the most sweet and delightful and edifying passages in the gospels and the epistles, already prepared to our hand.* All that is necessary is to versify, for example, such admirable passages as that of "the prodigal son," or any similar passage, and we have a most precious and affecting hymn of praise. And so with the deeply impressive scenes of the crucifixion: what heart can fail to relish, what tongue tenderly to respond to the narrative of the thief expiring on the cross, and turning his dying eyes upon the Saviour—"Lord, remember me." And then the sweet answer of the compassionate Redeemer—"This day thou shalt be with me in Paradise." And if we open the apostolic epistles, everywhere the holy raptures of the writers break forth in beautiful ascriptions of praise: "Unto the King eternal, immortal, invisible, the only wise God, be honor and glory forever and ever, amen." Or take Paul's sublime argument for the resurrection, in 1 Corinthians 15 : 51–58—"For this corruptible must put on incorruption, and this mortal put on immortality; * * * then shall be brought to pass the saying that is written, Death shall be swallowed up in victory.

O death where is thy sting?
O grave where is thy victory?

The sting of death is sin, and the strength of sin is the law. But thanks be to God who giveth us the victory through our Lord Jesus Christ." These are noble specimens of the Psalmody of the New Testament. They are *made* to our hand, and we ask no better. A volume at least twice as large as the "book of Psalms" can readily be gathered from this magnificent treasury of Di-

* "We find in them (the apostolical epistles,) abundance of *very suitable matter* for instruction, meditation, prayer and *praise*. When they are carefully looked into and examined with any degree of attention, we find there many *divine odes* and *sacred doxologies*." "The four evangelists yield * * * much *matter of praise*; * * therein we find several Divine songs and very *suitable matter for Divine hymns*."—Editor's Preface to the Works of Erskine, vol. 10, pp. 627, 644.

vine truth. * And then we have, besides, all that is most rich and grand and instructive and animating in the Psalms, Isaiah and all the prophets. Let hundreds of such passages as those we have cited, be paraphrased and versified with even the large license of many of the Psalms by Rouse, and we will have a volume of praise such as might fire the souls even of the ransomed in glory. "No book of Psalms in the New Testament!" We have what is far better—we have all that David and Asaph and Isaiah and the others wrote, illuminated by the brighter glories of the Sun of Righteousness, "who hath brought life and immortality to light through the gospel." We have all that the seraphic Paul, and the heavenly-minded John, and the golden-mouthed Luke ("the beloved physician"), and the ardent lion-hearted Peter — what shall I say! — we have *the very words* of Him who was goodness, and mercy, and virtue, and wisdom, all embodied in the incomparable person of the Son of God! Surely the church would be hard to satisfy, if she could ask more than this!

But hark! It is the voice of the objector—"Your New Testament hymns *are a serious corruption* of the worship of God! We *dare not* sing them, lest we should offer *strange fire* before the Lord!" Yet this is the language of ministers of the gospel, who profess great respect, yea, profound *reverence*, for the words of inspiration! Strange! O prejudice! How blind art thou!

* Many beautifnl specimens may be seen in the hymn book of the United Presbyterian church of Scotland, sixty-five of which are by Dr. Watts.

LETTER IX.

"A MORE EXCELLENT WAY"—WHOLE WORD OF GOD OF USE TO DIRECT US IN PRAISE—ACTS OF OUR SUPREME JUDICATORY—LABORS OF RALPH ERSKINE—EXTRACT FROM NORTH BRITISH REVIEW IN COMMENDATION OF DR. WATTS—HIS LABORS IN PSALMODY—HE VIEWED HIS VERSIFICATION AS A PARAPHRASE, NOT ALWAYS A STRICT TRANSLATION—MANY OF HIS PSALMS ARE CORRECT VERSIONS, AS REALLY AS ROUSE IN SAME PSALMS—SPECIMENS OF WATTS' MANNER, STERNHOLD AND HOPKINS—PSALMS NEED EXPOSITION—TESTIMONY OF PROF. PATTERSON.

MY DEAR SIR:—Having in previous Letters stated the principle adopted by our brethren in the matter of Psalmody, and given numerous illustrations of their practice under it, we are now prepared to exhibit, somewhat at large, "a more excellent way."

Receiving, as we do, "the whole word of God as of use to direct us" in his praise, no less than "in prayer" and the other parts of worship, we cannot adopt the theory which limits the church under her present dispensation to a small, though very precious collection of Psalms originally given to the Jews for a part of their temple service. Still less can we accept an explanatory paraphrase of those Psalms as "the very songs which God has given," "the veritable songs of inspiration in a *fair* and *literal* translation." To do this would be to deny the plainest evidence of our senses, to call black *white*, and white *black*, "to put bitter for sweet, and sweet for bitter." What, then, have we to show as "the more excellent way?"

If we were compelled to accept the judgment of those who oppose us, our cause must be desperate indeed. We will copy, for the amusement of the reader, a few of the curious epithets by which they attempt to disparage the Psalmody of our branch of the church. "Loose paraphrases," "modern hymns," "productions of an English poet," "hymns of mere human invention," "entire rejection, and impious rejection of the Psalms which God has given to his church to be sung," "mere effusions of men," "man-made Psalm book," "impious license taken with the book of Psalms," "preference of a human to a Divine book of Psalms," "exclusion of Scripture songs," "Psalm book prepared by man," "songs of human composure," "Watts' whymes," "confusion of Babel," &c. These specimens are selected from the most respectable authors on that side of the question.

But we are not to be silenced by declamation. Railing convinces nobody. We propose the only safe test in such cases, viz. an appeal to the record and to facts.

I. It is an undeniable fact that our Supreme Judicatory have, by a standing rule, often repeated but never repealed, authorized the use of Rouse's versification of the Psalms Thus, in 1787, after "allowing the use of Watts as revised by Barlow," they say, "we are at the same time FAR FROM DISAPPROVING *of Rouse's version*, commonly called 'the old Psalms,' in those who are in the use of them and choose to continue; * * * and do highly *disapprove* of severe and unchristian censures being passed upon either of said systems of Psalmody."

Now as in the judgment of these brethren, "Rouse's paraphrase" is "the songs of inspiration," this action of the Supreme Court of the Presbyterian church certainly does not look like "an impious rejection of the Psalms!" "We are far from disapproving of *Rouse's version.*"

The men who constituted the first Presbytery of our church (1705) were emigrants from Scotland and Ireland. They brought their Psalmody with them, and being endeared to them by recollections of home and similar associations, they were not likely to make any hasty changes in that department of worship. But the mother churches of Scotland had never adopted the modern *exclusive* principle which is so zealously defended in this country.*

* This appears from several considerations:

1. From the earliest specimens sung by the Scottish martyrs and reformers, and which were anything but "literal translations" of the Psalms.

And their children entertained the same liberal and broad views in founding and rearing the Presbyterian church.

Hence, when in the lapse of three quarters of a century (1706–1787), by the blessing of God on their labors, they had greatly multiplied—when in the ordinary revolution of language, manners, customs, &c., it was found highly important to have some improvement in Psalmody, they would naturally call to mind the acts of the Scottish General Assembly in 1647 and in 1701–7, for "examining the *other Scripture songs* by Zachary Boyd and by Patrick Sympson," those versified by the latter "having been *recommended* by that Assembly (1701) to be used in private families, in order *to prepare them for the public use of the church.*" And these early Presbyterians well knew that in 1747 the Associate or Antiburgher Presbytery of Scotland had recommended the celebrated Ralph Erskine "to versify the other Scripture songs," which labor he accomplished, quoting in his "preface" to the volume the action of the church of Scotland, as follows:

"The work of turning *all the rest of the Scripture songs* into metre, as the Psalms of David are, and *for the same public use,* was proposed by the church of Scotland, more than one hundred years ago, and that *in one of the most noted periods of reformation;* particularly by an Act of Assembly, August 28th, 1647."

2. The first complete versification (Sternhold and Hopkins') was a *broad paraphrase,* mingled with New Testament explanations, and embraced two Doxologies of mere "human composure."

3. The churches of Scotland long since authorized, and constantly have in use, a volume of *sixty-seven* paraphrases of "other parts of Scripture," to which are appended five or six pure hymns from Addison and others.

4. From "Stewart's Collections" we learn, that by the 15th Act of April, 1708, the Commission of the Assembly was "instructed and appointed to consider the printed version of the Scripture songs," (not the Psalms,) "with the remarks of the Presbyteries thereupon, and after examination thereof they were authorized and empowered to conclude and emit the same, *for the public use* of the church; the present version of the Psalms" (that is, Rouse's,) "having been ordered in the *same manner,* in the year 1649."

Nor were these early Presbyterians ignorant that the same Ralph Erskine had regarded his labors upon "the other Scripture songs," as an important addition to the Psalmody of the Associate church. Thus he remarks:

"As the poems and songs here written, are in the form of what is called rhyme and common metre, so the reason thereof is, to answer the design proposed to me, of making the Scripture songs adapted to the common tunes, so as it may be practicable *to sing them as we do the Psalms of David.*"

Again, in his preface to the "Song of Solomon," he says, after quoting Ephesians 18 : 19, and Colossians 3 : 16—"That you may be the more *able to sing it* ('the song') over with understanding, I have endeavored to lay open its mysteries," &c.

Again, he says he put his verse in "common metre," that "in case any should see fit to make some of these lines a part of their spiritual and devout recreation in secret, they might, if they please, *sing them over* in any of the tunes to which they are accustomed in our Scottish church." This refers to *secret worship*—but the "Testimony" of our brethren includes "worship both public and private."

With such antecedents and authorities as these, it was to be expected that the Presbyterian church in this country should early take decided action for the improvement of her Psalmody. Accordingly, under the leadership of Dr. Witherspoon, (*clarum et venerabile nomen,*) Dr. Rodgers, and men of like spirit, the act of our Supreme Judicatory quoted above, was passed, so far as appears on the records, without *a dissenting voice.*

This action of our highest church court is viewed by the brethren we oppose, as a "*preference of a human to a Divine* book of Psalms"—"an impious license," calling for Divine rebuke. But the facts are all against them. In the year 1705, our church consisted of seven ministers, and two or three years later they reported *ten* small congregations, numbering probably less than one thousand communicants. We pass on three-quarters of a century, during all which term Rouse's versification is, with almost no exception, exclusively the Psalmody of the church. She now (1787) reports thirteen Presbyteries and one hundred and sixty-three ministers, with probably two hundred congregations. The increase has been great, and she has reason to triumph in her God and King. But we pass over another three-fourths of a century, during all which time the church lies under the guilt of "an *impious rejection* of God's Psalm book." How stands the same church now, 1858? To the everlasting praise of her ascended Saviour be it spoken—she now numbers one hundred and fifty-nine Presbyteries, two thousand four hundred and sixty-eight ministers, three thousand three hundred and twenty-four churches, and more than two hundred and sixty thousand church members—while during the single year which terminated last May, she received to her communion from the world, twenty thousand seven hundred and ninety-two hopeful converts. At the same time, in all that constitutes purity, unity, Christian activity and usefulness, she is not a whit behind the very chief of the embattled hosts of God's elect, " her enemies themselves being judges." We say it in no spirit of boasting, but we trust with profound humility and dependence on Divine grace. FACTS like these do not show a church *forsaken* of her Almighty King! At the same rate of increase, it will require less than *three* years to swell her membership by an accession eight thousand greater than the sum total of the late Associate and Associate Reformed churches, now united in one body.

It is impossible at this late day, to ascertain minutely the motives which induced Dr. Witherspoon, and the other ministers and elders of our church, to seek an improved Psalmody. In the Act cited above there is not the remotest hint of any *hostility* to the precious "book of Psalms." Even of Rouse's antiquated versification they say they "*are far from disapproving.*" They did not allege that "an *uncouth version* (Rouse's) had put David's Psalms out of the church, and it would *keep them out.*" * We do not read that they urged *the duty and necessity* of an improved version, as Dr. Cooper does, because "no man of any *taste* and scholarship can fail to feel so." Nor yet in the words of Dr. Beveridge—"It must require a strong love for the inspired Psalms to overcome *the distaste* which would otherwise be felt to the language in which they are sometimes clothed, *especially by young persons and strangers.*"

These were doubtless regarded by such men as Witherspoon and Rodgers as matters of considerable interest—but we have reason to believe that they felt as their forefathers did, and especially such men as the judicious editor of Ralph Erskine's works, who penned the following:

"Though the Psalms of David are truly excellent and sublime, containing suitable matter for praise and adoration, &c., yet there are many passages in them peculiarly adapted *to the old dispensation of carnal* rites and ceremonies, and on that account, *cannot be supposed to be so clear and full of the grace and spirit of the gospel.* The consideration hereof hath induced many devout and piously disposed persons, ardently and sincerely to wish *that our Psalmody were enlarged,* not only by adding some other Scripture songs out of the Old Testament, but particularly by selecting a number from the New."

It is on such broad and liberal principles as these that our church has always acted. They could adopt, in part at least, the language of Dr. John Owen, whose name is a tower of strength in theology. He says: "*There was a promise of eternal life given to the saints under the Old Testament: but whereas they were obliged to a worship that was carnal and outwardly pompous,* they never had clear and distinct apprehensions of the future state of glory: for life and immortality were brought to light by the gospel."

* Rev. W. Davidson, of the United Presbyterian church.

Believing that there are brighter displays of the "excellent glory" in the New than in the Old Testament, they felt it to be a duty to use the clearer light, no less in the ordinance of *praise*, than in the other exercises of worship. We are far from "an impious setting aside of the Psalms which God has given, and using in their stead the *mere productions of men*," * as is rashly affirmed to our prejudice.

II. We are now prepared to examine the *improvements* which our church has authorized; and this is the more necessary, as it is especially upon these that our brethren direct the chief battery of their denunciations. The main instrument in preparing "the Psalms and Hymns" as we now use them, was the celebrated Dr. Isaac Watts.† A few years subsequent to the organization of the first Presbytery of our church (1705), Dr. W. published his system of Psalmody, perhaps 1708. Of the position which the "Psalms and Hymns" versified by Dr. W. maintain in the Free church of Scotland and the sister denominations, we cannot give a better idea than in the appended extracts from the "North British Review,"‡ which was founded by Chalmers, and is sustained by the leading men of the Free church: "A century and a half has nearly passed," says the Review, "since the publication of Dr. Watts' Psalms and Hymns; yet nothing has appeared to dim their lustre; as yet nothing threatens to supersede them. With their doctrinal fullness, their sacred fervor, their lyric grandeur, they stand alone, overtopping all their fellows." "To elevate to poetic altitudes every truth in Christian experience and revealed religion, needs the strength and sweep of an eagle's wing; and this is what Isaac Watts has done. He has taken almost every topic which exercises the understanding and the heart of the believer, and has not only given it a de-

* Rev. Dr. Kerr, editor of the Preacher. That our church feels no aversion to the system of Rouse, is obvious, in that she has lately added fifty selections from it to her Psalmody, as most commonly used.

† Born 1674; died 1748.

‡ For August, 1857.

votional aspect, but has wedded it to immortal numbers; and, whilst there is little to which he has not shown himself equal, there is nothing which he has done for mere effect. They are naturalized through all the Anglo-Saxon world, and, next to Scripture itself, are the great vehicle of pious thought and feeling." Again, says the same high authority: "A climbing boy was once heard singing in a chimney,

'The sorrows of the mind
Be banished from this place.
Religion never was designed
To make our pleasures less.'

And, like King David's own Psalter, the same strains which cheered the poor sweep in the chimney, and melted to tears the Northamptonshire peasants, have roused the devotion or uttered the rapture of ten thousand thousand worshipers; and there is many a reader who, in his experience, can imagine nothing more akin to celestial enjoyment, than the sensations which he shared in singing, when the heart of some solemn assembly was uplifted as one man, 'Come, let us join our cheerful song,' or, 'Jesus shall reign where'er the sun.'"

The contrast between this high eulogy from the pen of one of the gifted sons of the "Free church of Scotland," and the abusive *epithets* near the beginning of this Letter, is curious enough. But our safest course is, "to search the record," as the lawyers say, and thus ascertain for ourselves where the truth lies.

III. The judgment formed by Dr. Watts, in regard to his poetical labors, may be gathered from his own words. He frequently describes his versification as a "paraphrase." Thus: "Whensoever there shall appear any *paraphrase* of the book of Psalms that retains more of the savor of David's piety, and discovers more of the style and spirit of the gospel, * * * let this attempt of mine be buried in silence." Whether he is more or less paraphrastic than *Rouse*, is of course another question, which is not now under discussion.

Again, Dr. W. employs the general title, "The Psalms of David, imitated in the language of the New Testament, and applied to the Christian state and worship." His meaning is indicated as follows: "Where the Psalmist speaks of sacrificing goats or bullocks, I rather choose to mention the sacrifice of Christ, the Lamb of God. When he attends the ark with shouting into Zion, I sing the ascension of my Saviour. * * * Why should I now address my God and Saviour in a song with burnt sacrifices of fatlings, and with the incense of rams, * * * why should I bind my sacrifices with cords to the horns of the altar?" &c.

Again: In a letter* dated March 17th, 1718, and addressed to the eminently pious Dr. Cotton Mather, of New England, and in which he submitted some specimens of his labors in Psalmody, Dr. Watts writes as follows: "It is not a translation of David I pretend, but an imitation of him so nearly in Christian (or gospel) hymns that the Jewish Psalmist *may plainly appear*, yet leave Judaism behind."

From this extract two things are plain:

1. Dr. W. did not design to *exclude* David from the Psalmody of the church; on the contrary, he says he aimed to make him "*plainly appear*," yet without "Judaism."

2. In the phrase "Christian hymns," he obviously intended such a use of the terms as when we speak of "the Christian (or gospel) dispensation," in opposition to the "Jewish economy." This also shows what he means when he sometimes uses the objectionable phraseology, "teach David to speak like a *Christian*, or the common sense (or experience) of a Christian." He evidently means the opposite of *Jewish* experience. So in referring to translators of the Psalms, he says: "They taught the Hebrew Psalmist *to speak English*." But how unfair would it be to represent Dr. W. as teaching that the Holy Spirit, the real author of the Psalms, did *not*

* Published in the Boston Recorder, and certified by the editors.

understand the English language! Such a misrepresentation would be scouted by every candid and honorable mind, and must recoil upon its authors. Yet very much such usage has Dr. W. received from certain writers! "What need is there," he exclaims, "that I should wrap up the shining honors of my Redeemer in the dark and shadowy language of a religion which is now forever abolished; especially since Christians are so vehemently warned by Paul "against a Judaizing spirit?" His object was, as he himself affirms, "to change the dark expressions, and the Levitical ceremonies and Hebrew forms, into the worship of the gospel;" * * * and he adds, "thus should I rejoice to see *a good part* of the book of Psalms fitted for the use of the churches and David converted into a Christian." We do not defend the use of such phraseology, because it is very liable to be misunderstood; but when interpreted agreeably to the commonest rules of candor, it conveys no objectionable sense to any intelligent mind. Indeed, Dr. W. in these sentences, proposes to do with David precisely what every minister does, when from the pulpit he *explains* to the people these typical expressions, and teaches them to sing them as interpreted by the light of the gospel! If such a minister *explains the Psalms* correctly, he will, in most such cases, put *into the hearts of his people* (whatever may be in their lips,) just the admirable sense and import of these Jewish ceremonies as they are happily *explained and versified by Dr. Watts!* It is thus these Associate and Associate Reformed ministers "convert David into a Christian!" The heinous crime in the one case, is no less shocking than in the other; the chief difference being this — the one (Dr. Watts) sins in good poetry; the other (the preacher) sins in plain prose! And in singing such hymns, the devout Christian does what is enjoined in the Directory of the Associate Reformed church — "in singing those parts of them [the Psalms] which are expressed in the *ceremonial style,* or describe the *circumstances of the writers,* or of the *church* *in ancient times*, we *should* have our eye upon the *general principles* which are *implied* in them, and which are *applicable* to individuals or to the church in every age." Book 3, Ch. 3, Sec. 3.

IV. We are now prepared to take another step in the discussion. Every one familiar with his Bible, knows that of the compositions of "the sweet Psalmist of Israel," many have nothing of "Judaism" about them. They are beautiful expressions of that heaven-born piety, which is the same at all times and everywhere, whether among Jews or Gentiles. How does Dr. Watts deal with this class of Psalms?

We reply, he very generally gives correct *versions* of such Psalms; for example, the first, the twenty-third, the hundredth, &c. In this large and very precious class of sacred songs, he generally gives quite as correct a *version as Rouse*, and incomparably superior in all that constitutes poetry. This assertion may possibly surprise some persons who have been taught to regard our Psalmody, in the words of Rev. Dr. Kerr, of the "Preacher," as "the *mere* productions of men." But we again appeal to the record. Here is Dr. Watts' own account of the matter: In speaking of "the true method" of preparing the Psalms for New Testament worship, he says: "Psalms that are purely doctrinal or merely historical, are subjects for our meditation, and *may* be translated for our present use *with no variation*, if it were possible; and in general, ALL THOSE SONGS of Scripture which the saints of following ages *may assume for their own;* such as the 1st, the 8th, the 19th, and *many others*." We had intended to give a series of illustrations of this principle, copied from the Psalmody of our church—but for want of space, we confine ourselves to one specimen, the 100th Psalm, placing the prose of our Bibles in parallel column with the versification of Dr. Watts, as follows:

Make a joyful noise unto the Lord, all ye lands.	Ye nations round the earth, rejoice Before the Lord, your sovereign king.

Serve the Lord with gladness.	Serve him with cheerful heart and voice,
Come before his presence with singing.	With all your tongues his glory sing.
Know ye that the Lord he is God: it is he that made us, and not we ourselves; we are his people, and the sheep of his pasture.	The Lord is God; 'tis he alone Doth life and health and being give. We are his work, and not our own, The sheep that on his pasture live.
Enter into his gates with thanksgiving, into his courts with praise; be thankful to him and bless his name.	Enter his gates with songs of joy; With praises to his courts repair. And make it your divine employ To pay your thanks and honors there.
For the Lord is good; his mercy is from everlasting: and his truth endureth to all generations.	The Lord is good, the Lord is kind; Great is his grace, his mercy sure. And the whole race of men shall find His truth from age to age endure.

The right column, it will be seen, contains a very fair version of a precious inspired song of praise. It is much nearer a "correct and faithful version" than two-thirds of Rouse's paraphrases; and on the principles of our brethren, is therefore more strictly and truly "an inspired Psalm." Yet in addition to this large class of purely devotional songs, Dr. W. says, "he designed to make *no variation* in the purely doctrinal and historical Psalms." All these, therefore, if Dr. W. executed his purpose, are "the songs which God has given," not "the mere effusions of men," not "hymns of mere human invention," as our brethren rashly assert!

V. It was the express design of Dr. W. "wherever he found the person and offices of our Lord Jesus Christ in prophecy, to translate them in a way of history;" and he adds, "such evangelical truths should be stript of their veil of darkness," &c. When, for example, he read in Psalm 40 : 6, "Mine ears hast thou opened,"—he added with the apostle, "A body hast thou prepared me," &c. But such a use of New Testament light is quite offensive to our brethren, savoring of "impious license with the Psalms," "attempting to write better than David," &c. But it is remarkable that in her earliest, her martyr

Psalmody, the church of Scotland employed this very principle, i. e., she accommodated the Psalms to New Testament forms. Open the versification by Sternhold and Hopkins, which was used by that honored church for an hundred years before *Rouse* was thought of. Let us look at a few specimens of this "gospel turn." How is this matter managed in the second Psalm? Omitting some examples quoted in another Letter, pass to verse 12th: "When his wrath is kindled but a little, blessed are all they that put their trust in him."

STERNHOLD.	DR. WATTS.
If once his wrath never so small	If once his wrath arise,
Shall kindle *in his breast:*	Ye perish on the place;
O then all they that trust in Christ	Then blessed is the soul that flies
Shall *happy be* and blest.	For refuge to his grace.

Did the Church of Scotland imagine that such a use of the Psalms was "impious?" But take another example: "The kings of the earth set themselves, and the rulers take counsel together against the Lord, and against his anointed."

STERNHOLD.	DR. WATTS.
The kings and rulers of the earth	Why did the Gentiles rage,
Conspire *and all are bent*	And Jews with one accord,
Against the Lord and Christ *his Sonne,*	Bend all their counsels to destroy
*Which he amongst us sent.**	The anointed of the Lord.

This is another illustration of what Dr. Watts means by "converting David into a Christian." Sternhold and the church of Scotland practiced the same sort of *conversion!* Take a further illustration from David's beautiful penitential Psalm, the 51st, v. 7: "Purge me with hyssop, and I shall be clean: wash me, and I shall be whiter than the snow."

* "Where the original runs in the form of prophecy concerning Christ and his salvation, I have given a historical turn to the sense."—*Dr. Watts.*

STERNHOLD.	DR. WATTS.
If thou with hyssop purge *this blot* I shall be cleaner *than the glasse,* And if thou wash *away my spot,* The snow in whiteness I shall passe.	O wash my soul from every sin, And make my guilty conscience clean. No bleeding bird, nor bleeding beast, Nor hyssop branch, nor sprinkling priest, Nor running brook, nor flood, nor sea, Can wash the dismal stain away.

Again: observe the "gospel turn" in this: Psalm 87 : 5: "And of Zion it shall be said, This and that man was born in her; and the Highest himself shall establish her."

STERNHOLD.	DR. WATTS.
In their records to them it shall *Through God's device appeare,* Of Sion that the Chief of all Had his beginning there.*	Egypt and Tyre, and Greek and Jew, Shall there begin their lives anew; 'Twill be an honor to appear As one new born and nourished there.

Thus it will be seen, in accordance with the commentators, the venerable church of Scotland here fixes her eye upon "the Chiefest among ten thousand, the One altogether lovely," and is neither ashamed nor *afraid* to make the reference distinctly visible in her Psalmody.

We have room for only one additional example of this ancient Scottish "gospel turn." It is in Psalm 120 : 6–7 : "My soul hath long dwelt with him that hateth peace. I am for peace, but when I speak, they are for war."

STERNHOLD.	DR. WATTS.
With them that peace did hate *I came a peace to make* *And set a quiet life.* But when my tale is told, *Causeless I was controlde* By them that would have strife.	Peace is the blessing that I seek, How lovely are its charms! I am for peace—but when I speak They all declare for arms.

If only "a correct and faithful version" is of "Divine

* "I have often indulged the liberty of paraphrase, according to the words of Christ and his Apostles."—*Dr. Watts.*

appointment," neither of these versifications has very strong pretensions to it. But ours is quite a literal copy compared with Sternhold. Three lines of Sternhold's six are paraphrastic. Watts did not venture to give this a "gospel turn;" but Sternhold and Hopkins evidently had in their eye the New Testament history of Christ the "Prince of peace," who came "a peace to make" by "the blood of his cross." And both Bishop Horne and Dr. Scott in their comments, direct attention to "the Son of David, the Prince of peace," and Scott adds that here "David prefigured Christ." So thought the ancient church of Scotland, and accordingly arranges her Psalmody, so as to express this blessed truth.*

We could easily add to this list of "gospel turns," but we forbear. It thus appears that from the period of her first martyr, down to the Westminster Assembly (1643), the church of Scotland condemned in her practice the principle which requires "a correct and faithful version as of Divine appointment." It appears, moreover, that these variations from a faithful version or translation, were *designed, deliberate,* made on *principle,* and not at all accidental, or to be attributed to haste, carelessness, or the difficulty of constructing a versification in rhyme. Many of them are the very same sort of *studied departures* from the literal text for which our Psalmody has been so bitterly and unsparingly denounced; and in several instances, that venerable church, with her martyrs and other men of God, is demonstrated to have deliberately adopted and reduced to practice some of the very principles which lie at the basis of our system, and that in a more open, obvious "*impious*" manner and degree than was ever practiced even by Dr. Watts himself!

It is obvious, therefore, as is well remarked by Dr. Beveridge, that in the earliest metred Psalmody of that

* "What need is there that I should wrap up the shining honors of my Redeemer in the dark and shadowy language of a religion that is now for ever abolished." "What fault can there be in enlarging a little on the more useful subjects *in the style of the gospel,* (as Sternhold does,) where the Psalm gives any occasion."—*Dr. Watts.*

church, "*great liberties* were taken," and that these liberties were in numerous instances of the very same sort which Dr. Watts adopted in constructing his system of praise, much of which has been embodied in the Presbyterian Psalmody; and further, that those identical principles for which he has been most violently abused and denounced, are here incorporated and acted out by Sternhold, and practiced by the ancient Scottish church! Hence it follows, that in the structure of her Psalmody, the Presbyterian church, by rejecting the exclusive idea of "a correct and faithful *version* of the whole book of Psalms," has only returned to the safe precedent and pure practice of the noblest and best church of the Protestant Reformation, in the days of her greatest glory. The principle is the same in both systems, though it has been more extensively introduced in our Psalmody than in theirs. Both equally reject "the Divine right" of "a correct and faithful version of the Psalms"—in both the *right* and duty are recognized and deliberately reduced to practice, viz. to deviate in various methods and on all suitable occasions, from "a correct and faithful version." The illustrations which might be brought forward from the system of praise adopted by that noble old Presbyterian church, would fill many pages, since more or less of the same additions, omissions, historic amendments, exegetical comments, "gospel turns," &c., might be collected from nearly every page.

We pause here. Enough has been said to enable every one to decide whether "the songs contained in the book of Psalms are virtually excluded from the worship of the (Presbyterian) church."* In view of such facts and reasonings as the foregoing, was it worthy of these brethren to publish our church as "shoving God's hymn-book aside, and substituting *one made by ourselves*—laying aside a God-written book, except *two short hymns*, and using in its place a man-written book," which they interpret to mean that "a mere man (Dr. Watts, for example,) *has*

* Dr. Pressly, in the Preacher, September 27, 1844.

written a better book than God." * Certainly Dr. Watts never exposed himself to any such imputations, since his avowed object was, "that the Jewish Psalmist (i. e., his inspired sentiments,) should PLAINLY APPEAR, yet leave Judaism behind." †

VI. Before I close this Letter, another topic demands a moment's attention. Is there any great importance to be attached to the explanatory and paraphrastic improvements introduced by our Scottish forefathers, and extended in our Psalmody? Was there *a necessity* for such explanations of parts of the Psalms? We answer:

1. Bishop Horne, in the preface to his commentary, remarks—"Is it not to be feared that for want of such instructions (expositions, &c.) the repetition of the Psalms, as performed by multitudes, is but *one degree above mechanism.*" Dr. Watts states this thing in various forms, and undertook his versification for the *avowed purpose* of remedying this sore evil.

2. Our brethren themselves in effect concede all that is asserted by Bishop Horne. They adopt the practice of *explaining the Psalm* before the people sing it, at least one Psalm each Sabbath—the others they leave unexplained. Now why is this *explanation* thought to be very important? One writer says, "It is to stir up devotional feelings, and prepare the worshipers to engage in praising God with suitable affections." ‡ But is that all? Hear Prof. Patterson || in the "Westminster Herald," February, 1855. He says—"*The Psalms require exposition.*" "That all *may sing profitably* for personal and

* United Presbyterian, March, 1851.

† We quote Dr. Watts' express declarations. "*Far be it from* my thoughts," he says, "TO LAY ASIDE THE BOOK OF PSALMS IN PUBLIC WORSHIP; few can pretend so *great a value for them* as myself. It is the most artful, most devotional and *Divine* collection of poesy; and nothing can be supposed more proper to raise a pious soul to heaven, than some parts of that book; never was a piece of experimental divinity so nobly written and so justly reverenced."

‡ Pressly on Psalmody, p. 25.

|| See an article signed P. of date as above. Prof. P. is an able minister of the United Presbyterian church.

mutual edification, they must *understand them.*" "People who hardly ever hear them explained KNOW NOTHING *of their spiritual worth.*" He says, "he has viewed the decline of the good old-fashioned plan of *expounding* a part of the Psalm, with feelings of deep solicitude"—and adds, that it is "a manifest declination from duty." "Shall these well-springs of the God of Israel be CLOSED and SEALED?" These expressions are more than Dr. Watts ever ventured to say on that topic. Prof. P. is thus full and explicit, though we do not see why his remarks do not apply with equal force to the five other Psalms sung each Sabbath, as well as to the first one used at the morning service, which alone is explained. It is not necessary to maintain that the people *sing the minister's explanations,*—they sing "Rouse's paraphrase," putting the minister's *explanations* on the words. The Presbyterian system embodies "the explanations," not in all the Psalms, but in all cases in which they are needed, *in the poetry itself.* They are usually "the explanations" of our best commentators put into smooth verse. If both parties "sing with the spirit and understanding also," as Paul requires, both employ the same sentiments, the chief difference consisting *only in the form of words,* whether of Rouse or Dr. Watts.

LETTER X.

ATTEMPTS TO CREATE PREJUDICE BY REFERENCE TO THE SENTIMENTS OF DR. WATTS — HOW FAR PRESBYTERIANS ARE RESPONSIBLE FOR HIS STATEMENTS — GREATLY MISREPRESENTED — HIS HIGH APPRECIATION OF THE BOOK OF PSALMS — EXAMINATION OF SUNDRY OBJECTIONS —"OMISSIONS"—"WATTS WROTE BETTER THAN DAVID"—"OUR PSALMODY NOT THE WORD OF GOD"—"TENDS TO WEAKEN THE CLAIMS OF INSPIRATION"—"THOSE WHO USE ROUSE, CERTAINLY SING THE TRUTH"—"DARE NOT SING HUMAN COMPOSITION," &C. &C.

MY DEAR SIR:—In reading the ablest treatises by our brethren, one thing must have struck every candid mind with surprise, viz. the labored effort they make to arouse prejudice and create odium by certain quotations from "the essay" and "prefaces" of Dr. Watts. We are repeatedly told that "the imitation" was introduced to public notice in this country by "prefaces" containing *bitter libels* against the songs of Zion, and that it was recommended by those sentiments," and "the arguments *most popular* and *frequently* used, represent these Divine compositions (the Psalms) as Christless." *

But surely it requires no proof to show that the essay and prefaces of Dr. W. are of no authority in our church. She has never indorsed, nor even printed them. So far as has come under the notice of the writer, they have never been *reprinted in this country;* and therefore are very rarely to be met with, except in the fragmentary extracts found in certain books on Psalmody! In preparing the materials for these Letters, we searched in vain every library to which we could gain access in Pittsburgh; and at last were successful in finding a copy of Dr. Watts' works, only in the library of a gentleman who had brought it from Europe. The Presbyterian church, as intimated in another Letter, has never adopted many of the sentiments and suggestions of that writer, exhibiting

* Apology, p. 77.

his reasons for certain changes in the Psalms. They are *his reasons,* not ours. This is true even when these reasons are understood in their most favorable sense—and especially so, when, as we maintain, they *are perverted* to mean what is notoriously contrary to his deliberate and oft repeated declarations. As to their being *common* and *popular* arguments in defense of our Psalmody, nothing is more opposed to the truth. The writer of these pages was for more than *twenty-five* years a member of the Presbyterian body, and never once met with the documents referred to, except in M'Master's Apology, and this we know to be a common experience both among our ministry and membership. Indeed, if some objectionable expressions of Dr. Watts' "essay and prefaces" had not been carefully published and disseminated by these brethren, for the avowed purpose of prejudicing the cause of a New Testament Psalmody, they would have been *dead and forgotten* long ago. Upon *their* heads, not upon ours, must rest the blame, whatever it may be, of keeping certain injudicious phraseology used by Dr. Watts before the public mind.

But Dr. W. is charged with having uttered "bitter libels against the songs of Zion." We have never met with anything from his pen, which, on a *fair* construction, could justify such an assertion. Dr. W. is not commonly accused with wanting common sense — yet he must have been little less than *crazed* if he could have been guilty of such profane and wicked conduct, while in the same pages he wrote as follows: "I esteem the book of Psalms as the most valuable part of the Old Testament, on many accounts. I advise the reading and meditation of it more frequently than any single book of Scripture; *and what I advise I practice. Nothing is more proper* to furnish our souls with devout thoughts and lead us into a world of spiritual experiences. The expressions of it that are not Jewish or peculiar, give us constant assistance in prayer and in praise."

Again, I quote Dr. W.: "Although there are many

gone before me who have taught the Hebrew Psalmist to speak English, (translators,) yet I think I may assume this pleasure, of being the first who hath brought down the royal author into the common affairs of the Christian (in opposition to Jewish) life, and *led the Psalmist of Israel into the church* of Christ without anything of a Jew about him." "My design was that the Jewish Psalmist *should plainly appear*, yet leave Judaism behind."

Another quotation from Dr. Watts: "I confess it is not unlawful nor absurd for a person of knowledge and skill to sing *any part* of the Jewish Psalm book, and consider it merely as the word of God, from which, by wise meditation, he may draw some inferences for his own use. But when the words are obscure Hebraisms, or the poet personates a Jew, a soldier, or a king, speaking to himself or to God, this mode of instruction in a song seems not *so natural or easy*, even to the most skillful Christian, and it is almost impracticable to the *greatest part of mankind.*" Dr. W. is here explaining one chief principle in the formation of his system of Psalmody, and instead of proposing an "impious rejection of the Psalms," he assigns a most forcible and conclusive reason for the practice of "explaining the Psalm," before the congregation sing it.

I repeat, therefore, the man who could indite these and scores of similar paragraphs, must have been destitute of common sense, if in the same connections he could "*bitterly libel*" the precious book of Psalms. But as this is the most effective, certainly the most *popular*, of all the arguments of our opposing brethren, we defer some other illustrations of the treatment they give Dr. Watts to our closing Letter, No. XIV.

Let us now attend to some objections to our theory of Psalmody:

1. It is objected that "following Dr. Watts, we omit some parts of the book of Psalms." Very true. Our principle is that "the whole word of God is of use to

direct us" *in praise* as well as "in prayer." We regard some parts of the New Testament as suitable for praise. But what shall we say of Rouse's omissions, for example, the 20th verse of the 72d Psalm, and the greater part of the titles or inscriptions, which Horne and other standard writers admit to be parts of the inspired text, as really as the first verses of Isaiah and the Epistle to the Ephesians. You profess to regard the Psalms as "the inspired Psalter," given precisely in sum and substance as Divine Wisdom saw best, for purposes of praise—and yet you venture to make these *improvements* upon "God's Psalm book"—*to reject* a part of the Holy Scriptures, &c.!

Again: In his preface to the recent "improved version," published under direction of a committee of the Associate or Seceder church, Dr. Beveridge says: "In a few instances *things omitted* in our version (Rouse) have been restored. See, for example, Psalm 31 : 11; Psalm 37 : 35, 36; Psalm 62 : 1–5; Psalm 78 : 21; Psalm 128 : 2, 3." Here is the same dilemma. Professing to regard the one hundred and fifty Psalms as exclusively "God's Psalter," indited for this very purpose by the Infinite Mind and "appointed as the Psalmody of the church," as Dr. Pressly says, "in which God teaches his church how to praise," you *dare* to tamper with God's work; by omitting parts of God's *teaching*, you thus destroy the Divine completeness of the Psalm book composed and appointed by Infinite Wisdom!

On the principle adopted by these brethren, to omit any part of the book of Psalms *is to pretend to be wiser than God*, who gave it all to be the Psalm book of the church; and is nothing short of the impiety which "takes away from the word of God." We reject this view of the subject, believing that God has given his "whole word to direct us in praise"—and therefore we are no more obliged to sing every part of the Psalms, than to sing every *other part* of the inspired records. But this plea offers no excuse for these brethren's "omissions."

A parallel case is this: "All Scripture is given by inspiration of God, and is profitable for doctrine, reproof, instruction in righteousness." The reading of these Scriptures from the pulpit, is an ordinance of God as really as public praise. But are there not portions of the inspired writings which no man of common sense ever *dares* to read to the people? Why? Those parts of God's blessed word are not suitable to be read publicly, though anciently read in the synagogues — in that way they are not profitable for instruction in righteousness. Let any minister rise in the sacred desk and read, for example, some parts of the Levitical law — how many hearers would he have on the next Sabbath? How soon would he be called to account by his Presbytery, as lacking common sense! But does any one ever dream of this being an impious attempt *to be wiser than God?* Apply the same reasoning to the whole word of God considered as of use to direct us in praise as well as in prayer and reading—and everything is clear. And the same reasoning holds good in regard to the ordinance of preaching. Is not the whole inspired volume of use to direct us in this service? But there are certain texts which none but a fool would ever make the foundation of a sermon. Now in omitting certain parts of the Psalms as *less suitable* for praise than some other parts of the inspired volume outside of that book, we offer no reproach to any part of God's word, but do equal honor to all portions of the Divine volume, designed as they were for different uses in the church. If, indeed, there were any "Divine precept" to sing every jot and tittle of the Psalms, we would do it. So if there were a scriptural command to read publicly every text of the Bible, we would do that too!

2. It is objected that our system involves the daring implication, "that a mere man is able to improve 'God's Psalm book,' and 'to write better than the Holy Spirit.'"

This objection comes with a bad grace from those who

use "Rouse's paraphrase," with all its errors, omissions, additions, explanations, &c. For example:

> "I like an owl in desert am,
> Which nightly there doth moan."

The second line is a mere human *improvement*, an explanation (whether right or wrong) of what the Psalmist meant. Scores of these *improvements*, as we have already shown, are found in Rouse — therefore it follows that these brethren have thought they "could write better than the Holy Spirit!" Or at least they have attempted to *improve* upon "God's Psalm book."

3. Another objection: "You Presbyterians do not sing the word of God." But is Rouse the pure word of God? Is the second line above quoted found among "the words which the Holy Ghost teacheth?" There is an important scriptural sense, however, agreeably to which a large part of our Psalmody is "the word of God"—the sense in which Paul uses these terms when he exhorts, "Preach the word." Compare the method we adopt, with some other parts of Divine worship: Does the able lecturer on large passages of Scripture, *preach* the word of God? Does the minister who EXPLAINS THE PSALMS teach the word of God? True, it is sometimes TRANSPOSED, to increase the light to our feeble vision; sometimes too the preacher selects particular sections; sometimes when the same idea occurs frequently, he groups the verses together. At other times he will group texts from remote parts of the Bible, as the ground work of a particular sermon, and adduce his proofs and illustration from every accessible source of Holy Writ. Still this does not make it less "the word of God." So we say of the system of Psalmody used by the Presbyterian church. Dr. Watts has grouped with the Psalms much of the thought and language of the New Testament, but this mixture does not make it less truly "the word of God." We do not mean that the two things are in all respects the same or exactly paral-

lel, but in this particular point they are the same in principle. If then the sound minister "preaches the word in season, out of season," on the same principle we sing the word of God. If the same minister IN EXPLAINING THE PSALM, gives a correct interpretation, and teaches "the word of God," and the people sing with this explanation fresh in their minds, and forming the sentiments of their hearts; with equal certainty do we worship in the use of "the word of God." The language is but *sound*—the *worship* is the utterance of the SENTIMENTS OF THE HEART. If these latter are acceptable to God, because agreeable to Divine teaching, the worship is "in spirit and in truth," whether we sing the prose of the English translation of the Scriptures or poetry arranged by an uninspired man (Rouse), or an "imitation" in which "David (i. e., his INSPIRED SENTIMENTS) plainly appears," and types and shadows, bullocks, burnt offerings, trumpets, cornets, dances, &c., dissolve amid the blessed and transforming light of the gospel.

We do not plead that our system of Psalmody is perfect. Particular examples may possibly be adduced in which the great "principle" adopted by Dr. Watts, viz. "to make David (his inspired sentiments) plainly to appear" is imperfectly developed. But there are also gross errors in Rouse. Dr. Dwight has supplied the Psalms omitted by Dr. Watts; and if in a few others, certain parts are omitted, they no more vitiate the whole system than Rouse's blunders vitiate that used by our brethren. If any serious departures from our principle are discovered in our system, it is the province of our General Assembly to supply the defect.

In both systems it can be demonstrated that there is a number of Psalms which approach so near "a correct and literal version" of the original, as to entitle them to be regarded as "inspired songs of praise"—but it is no less true that, to a great extent, both Rouse and Watts are neither more nor less than "paraphrases." The one may be *more or less* paraphrastic than the other; but that alters not the principle. He that *strains* at Watts, while he readily *swallows* Rouse, will not be suspected of great consistency.

4. Fourth objection. The Presbyterian principle in Psalmody "tends to make the mind indifferent to the claims of inspiration." We maintain "that all Scripture being given by inspiration of God," it is lawful to sing any suitable part of it, whether of the Old or New Testament; and that the church has a Divine warrant for drawing the subjects of her praise from other parts of the word of God. Consequently, that she may and ought to derive much of her praise from the inspired writers of the New Testament, which has so much more clearly revealed the character, offices and work of Christ.

Now can any intelligent Christian inform us how such a "principle" tends to make men infidels? Instead of some things descriptive of Jewish rites and ceremonies now abolished and forbidden, events in some of the Jewish wars, (see Horne, Dr. Scott and others,) prayers for the destruction of the enemies of David as the king of the Jews, (see the commentators,) and some other matters of this kind which were highly appropriate to the Jews, but which probably would never have been thought of as literal matter of praise in the New Testament church, if found in any other part of the Holy Scriptures—instead of these we feel authorized by the word of God to sing the songs of Mary, Anna, Simeon, "the heavenly host," and in fine any suitable part of the New Testament. In addition, therefore, to the Psalms, we rejoice to praise God in the use of several hundred hymns, embracing the chief instructions delivered by the Blessed Redeemer and his apostles.

Would to God the whole world were full of such *infidelity* as this! We are perfectly sure that there is a much stronger tendency toward loose, infidel conceptions in another quarter. When ministers of the gospel speak of "Rouse's paraphrase" as the "inspired Psalms," "the very songs which God has given," "God's Psalm book," &c., it is an abuse of language leading directly to false and heretical views of inspiration, and accustoming the people to the low Socinian conceptions of Belsham and others, by applying that term to the patchwork of Rouse and others. This is a serious evil; nor does it "lean to virtue's side," but to the *side* of a most dangerous soul destroying heresy. If you teach the people to regard "Rouse's paraphrase" as the inspired Psalms, it would be quite easy for them to go a step further, and receive the doctrines of Priestly and his Unitarian followers.

It has been proved that Rouse's paraphrases are inspired just as the pulpit *explanations* at your morning service. We do not say this of a goodly number of his Psalms, which are quite closely and accurately versified, but only of his numerous paraphrases; and to speak of these as "the inspired Psalms," is to confound all distinction between that which is inspired and that which is uninspired—between human and Divine. Our brethren should look *at home*, when they inquire after tendencies to reject the doctrine of Divine inspiration.

5. Fifth objection. "In the exclusive use of the one hundred and fifty Psalms we may be confident *of singing the truth*, and of praising God with sentiments suitable and acceptable to Him." Let us test this statement. We go to the Synod of Ulster, Ireland, as it was some years since, where nothing but the one hundred and fifty-Psalms were used, and when the heresy of Arianism had well nigh swallowed up all the churches. We enter one of these Arian establishments. The minister rises and explains the second Psalm, informing the people that God's "only Son," his "anointed," is a mere creature of a very high order; that to "perish from the way," does not mean any thing more than some temporal evil, that hell is an Eastern fable, &c. With this *explanation* fresh in their minds, the congregation sing the Psalm. Do they "*praise God with sentiments suitable and acceptable to Him?*" In what correct sense do they

even "sing the truth." Their lips may utter the language of truth, but their hearts are filled with a subtle and soul destroying heresy. With their lips and language, they "draw nigh to God;" but what does the heart utter before Him—the answer is, falsehood and impiety.

It will not be pretended that even if our brethren sung *the prose* in our Bibles, the naked words would constitute "the truth." *The truth* is the Divine sentiment, *the thought*, not the verbiage. Then what is the *sentiment* of an Arian, who has just received and believes the "*explanation*" of his Arian pastor? Surely not the truth, but heresy, however correct the *words* which flow from his lips. So too the Jews in their synagogues sing the Psalms of David, the second among the rest. Do they too sing *the truth*, while cursing the Lord Jesus in their heart? We admit that it is no objection to any part of the Old Testament that it is read or sung by Jews and Arians. All that we now contend for is, that the fact of their thus reading or singing is no certain evidence that as *it is explained to them*, they either read or sing "the truth." They may read the *words* which contain the truth—but so do men often "draw nigh to God with their lips, while their heart is far from him." And we may safely affirm, that neither Arian nor Jew could be persuaded to join with the Presbyterians in singing these verses of Dr. Watts' paraphrase of the 2d Psalm:

The things so long foretold
By David, are fulfilled:
When Jews and Gentiles join to slay
Jesus, thine holy Child!

I call him my ETERNAL SON,
And raise him from the dead;
I make my holy hill his throne,
And wide his kingdom spread.

Be wise, ye rulers of the earth,
Obey the ANOINTED LORD;
Adore the King of heavenly birth,
And tremble at his word.

Or this,

Jesus, MY GOD, thy blood alone
Hath power sufficient to atone.
Thy blood can make me white as snow;
No Jewish types could cleanse me so.

Or this,

Aside the Prince of glory threw
His most Divine array,
And wrapped his GOD-HEAD in a veil
Of our inferior clay.

Presbyterians maintain that the Psalmody of the Christian church, like all her other institutions, should reflect the light of the New Testament, which no Jew will take into his hands, except *to spit upon it.* Why so? Because it so clearly reveals "Christ and his cross." It is not denied that good men have often communed with their Saviour in the Psalms—so they have found him in innumerable forms of the Levitical law. But that does not prove that in New Testament worship, all *further light* is needless! What would be thought of the preaching and the public prayers, which, in the absence of other evidence, would leave a stranger habitually *in doubt* whether he sat in the presence of Christians or Jews? Yet just so is it in public praise with the Old Testament Psalms, except as their "explanation" alters the case. We admit that there is much of Christ in them, and so was there in the Levitical sacrifices as types of "the Lamb of God." But does that prove that in either case the far brighter displays of Divine love and mercy under the gospel are needless to the church in her forms of public praise? No more than it proves them useless in preaching and prayer.

Suppose it should be truly reported of all the ministers who use exclusively the Old Testament Psalms, that their *preaching* and *public prayers* give no "testimony" such as would offend an Arian, or even a Jew, in regard to the Divinity and Messiahship of Christ. Would such a reputation be considered *a compliment?* What Christian church would seek for such pastors? Yet that very circumstance, which would expose their *preaching* and *prayers* to the rebuke of Paul, viz. that their "trumpet gives an *uncertain* sound"—this very deficiency which would exclude them from Christian pulpits, is found in their *system of praise!* The Arians of Ulster and the Jews everywhere gladly hold fellowship with them in the ordinance of praise, at least as often as they sing without a pulpit "explanation." Can this be the method in which the Lord Jesus requires us to "CONFESS HIM BEFORE MEN?" And this argument has special force against those who think it necessary to prepare and publish a pamphlet "Testimony" against their Presbyterian brethren—against "views and practices" which, they say, "*demand* of them such 'testimony' *as witnesses for the truth!*" And yet, in *five* parts out of every six of all their *public praise*, their "*trumpet* gives so uncertain a sound," their *testimony* for important truth is so feeble, that Jews and Arians hold communion with them! Is there not great inconsistency and error here?

It is no valid objection to this reasoning, that Arians and Jews pervert in like manner the whole Bible. The Jew indeed hates the New Testament, because it is so full of THE CROSS—but he receives the Old Testament. The Arian professes some sort of faith in both Testaments. But such is the blindness and wickedness of man, that even God's word, as it has pleased its glorious Author to give it to mankind, is found insufficient to exclude error from his church. Hence nearly all denominations form creeds and confessions of faith as a remedy for resulting evils, and our brethren add a formal "Testimony" to the Holy Scriptures and their Confession, to testify for the truth as they hold it.

Now why is all this? Obviously that they as "faithful witnesses for the truth," may make an open and intelligible protest against error, which they admit could not be done by simply taking the Bible, "the perfect law of God," as their creed and "Testimony." And what is the object of their preaching and their "explahations" of the Psalms? Plainly that they may be "valiant for the truth in the earth." The Bible, they concede, *needs* all these varied *ministrations* and helps, in order that error may be excluded and pure religion make progress, and finally and universally triumph. Yea, the Bible, God's perfect law, makes these additional ministrations of creeds, preaching, &c., *a solemn duty.* And by these methods the Arian and other soul destroying heresies are banished from the church. Thus in their creeds and testimonies, in reading and expounding the Scriptures and in public prayer, these brethren clearly and distinctly lift up a banner for the truth as they view it.

But there is one *strange* exception! In five parts of every six of their public praise, they are found deficient in testifying for the truth! Their trumpet gives "so uncertain a sound" that the Jew and the Arian can hold fellowship with them! While they lift up their voices together, in *five-sixths of their public praise* it is impossible to tell which is the Jew and which the Christian! The Jew, though bitterly hating Christ, joins in worship with the Christian, and finds nothing to offend him—the Arian, too, unites cheerfully in a worship which allows him to regard "God's own Son" only as an "exalted creature!" In five parts of every six, they praise God every Sabbath, in strains to which neither Jews nor Arians object! These brethren do not *thus* preach the gospel—they are not thus defective in other ministrations, such as the public exposition of the Scriptures and prayer. It is only in the ascription of praise that their "confession of the name of the Lord Jesus" is so indistinct, their trumpet gives so uncertain a sound, that the grossest errorists harmonize with the friends of the gospel. Can this be the sort of "testimony" which the blessed Saviour requires of them that offer praise?

It is idle to allege that we are "speaking reproachfully of the book of Psalms." Nothing is farther from the truth. We are saying of that admirable book precisely what you, by your creed and "Testimony," say of the whole Bible, viz. that it *demands* of the church certain additional explanatory forms of "witnessing for the truth," as bonds of harmony and tests of soundness in the faith, as well as ramparts against heresy. As a very precious portion of the holy oracles; as in part the text-book of the ministry; as an invaluable source of "learning," and comfort of the Scriptures, &c., the Psalms, like the whole Bible, are precisely what they ought to be, most excellent productions of Infinite Wisdom. But believing, as we do, the church to be "*the pillar and ground of the truth*," she is bound to *confess Christ* just as plainly and unequivocally in *praise*, as in preaching and prayer; and we, therefore, deny that "the book of Psalms" was designed by its Divine Author, especially in its literal and naked form, to be the only and all-sufficient volume of praise. And yet there are those, strange to tell, yea, ministers of the gospel, who *boast* of the anti-sectarian character of "Rouse's paraphrase," because, forsooth, Jews, Mormons, Unitarians, &c., can unite in singing it!

6. A sixth objection. "We dare not sing 'human composition' in the worship of God." Well, if any one can really persuade himself that dozens of "Rouse's paraphrases" are "inspired composition," we shall not attempt to reason with him. All who use Rouse are necessarily guilty of this sin.

7. "If some parts of the Psalms are unsuitable for praise, they are not fit to be read."

It is not necessary to pronounce any parts of the Psalms absolutely, and under all circumstances, *unfit* to be sung. Our doctrine is, that some portions of that book are *less suitable* to be sung under the present dispensation, than many *other* parts of the holy oracles. But do not our brethren maintain that large parts of *both* Testaments are unsuitable for public praise? Take the first chapter of 1st Chronicles—"Adam, Sheth, Enosh," &c. They will concede that this is not fit for public praise, and so of other whole books, except the one hundred and fifty Psalms. Are they therefore unfit to be read? Certainly God may speak to us in language which we may not speak to him.

8. "The 'imitation' by Dr. Watts, is not much more of an *imitation* of the Psalms, than Young's Night Thoughts, or Pollok's Course of Time." This extraordinary assertion has been deliberately printed and circulated, in at least *three* different forms within a few years. It furnishes a sad illustration of the extreme folly to which the *furor* of controversy will sometimes hurry otherwise serious and true men.

Having now finished all that I deemed necessary to vindicate Presbyterian usages in regard to the book of Psalms, in my next I propose to speak of "the other songs of Scripture," which our brethren call "*corruptions* of the ordinance of God," when sung in public and private worship.

LETTER XI.

HYMNS — THE HISTORY OF "OTHER SONGS OF SCRIPTURE" — USAGES OF MOST OF THE SCOTTISH CHURCHES, VIZ.: 2,800 TO 30 — ACTION OF THE EARLY FATHERS OF THE ASSOCIATE REFORMED CHURCH — DR. M'MASTER'S SENTIMENTS — PRESENT VIEWS OF DRS. KERR AND PRESSLY — A GLANCE AT THE LEGITIMATE RESULTS — A LARGE PART OF DR. WATTS' HYMNS ARE FAIR PARAPHRASES OF PORTIONS OF THE INSPIRED RECORD, AND NO MORE "HUMAN COMPOSITION" THAN ROUSE — DEFENSE OF THE REMAINDER.

MY DEAR SIR: — Before proceeding to discuss the merits of that large department of our Psalmody, viz. "the other scriptural songs," &c., a glance at the history of the subject may tend to its better elucidation In a former Letter reference was made to the directions given by the Scottish General Assembly of 1647, to "Zachary Boyd to translate the other scriptural songs in metre, * * * that after examination they may send the same to the Presbyteries." In 1648, "Master John Adamson and Mr. Thomas Crawford were directed to revise the labors of Zachary Boyd *upon the other scriptural songs*, * * * that after examination the same may be reported to the next General Assembly." In 1649, the Assembly ordered their commission for public affairs "to emit (Rouse's) paraphrase of the Psalms for public use;" but the labors of Z. Boyd do not seem have been authorized; and it is no matter of surprise. They appear to have possessed very small poetical merit. This history, however, clearly demonstrates that the Scottish Assembly even at that early day, were desirous of some improvement and extension of their Psalmody. Nor do they seem to have had any fear of committing a certain great sin!

Accordingly at a later date, that venerable church authorized and constantly prints in her Bibles, what she calls "translations and paraphrases of *several passages* of Scripture." They are seventy-two in number, the last five, however, being pure "hymns of human composition," not even professing to be founded on a passage of Holy Writ. These additions to "Rouse's paraphrase" are commonly annexed to the Psalms in metre, at the end of the Bible.

When the "Free church of Scotland" separated from the Establishment, they made no change in Psalmody. Accordingly, at the solemn funeral services of their Assembly in May, 1847, on occasion of the death of Dr. Chalmers, "the proceedings were commenced by the Moderator giving out the last three verses of the 53d paraphrase," not a Psalm of David:

> "The saints of God from death set free,
> With joy shall mount on high," &c.

Some of our brethren in this quarter, of course condemn such "an impious preference of an English poet over David" as tending to infidelity. In truth, these "translations and paraphrases" are mere hymns, for the most part founded on a passage of Scripture. Dr. Watts composed a number of them.

In regard to the *extent* to which "the use of other productions than the Psalms" is carried in the churches of Scotland, the following statement has been handed to the author by two gentlemen of great intelligence, and who are minutely familiar from personal knowledge, with the ecclesiastical usages in that country. It may be added that these figures refer to the year 1852. Probably some change may have occurred since that period. They say: "There are in Scotland one thousand three hundred congregations of the Established church, all of which make use of hymns and paraphrases, selected from the devotional poetry of Dr. Watts and others. There are eight hundred congregations of the Free church, all of which have the same practice. There are seven hundred congregations of the United Presbyterian church, and the same is their uniform practice. All of these do, however, make use of Rouse's versification of the Psalms. There is now no other body of Presbyterians than the above mentioned, except the Covenanters, and these consist of about thirty congregations, and even these do not all adopt the exclusive views." So that the proportion against *the exclusive* use of the Psalms of David, is as two thousand eight hundred to thirty.

One of the denominations referred to, is called the "United Presbyterian church of Scotland." It was formed by a union of the orthodox part of the Synod of Ulster (which had ejected the Arians,) with the Secession church. In September, 1847, we were told by the editor * of the "Preacher" of Pittsburgh, "that while the Arians departed farther and farther from a Scripture Psalmody, the orthodox of the Synod of Ulster became more and more attached *and confined to the inspired Psalms*, until the time of their union with the Secession church."

And again, by the same authority: "It is true, the exclusive use of the book of Psalms was not made a term of communion in the United church; but her *testi-*

* Rev. Dr. Kerr.

mony as a church, was in favor of the Psalms *exclusive ly*, the use of paraphrases being regarded then, as it is yet, a matter of toleration."

But our brethren are not always accurate in matters of this sort. We have had in our possession for several years, the "Hymn book of the United Presbyterian church," issued in Edinburgh. It consists of nearly five hundred songs of praise, and bears on the title page that old apostolic proof-text in favor of New Testament Psalmody, viz. "In psalms and hymns and spiritual songs, singing and making melody in your heart." Ephesians 5 : 19. One hundred and thirty-five of these hymns are the same with those in our Presbyterian system. About *seventy* are from the pen of Dr. Watts; and although this church retains Rouse, she has paraphrased one hundred and sixty-five passages of the old Psalms among her hymns! Could her testimony have been stronger in *favor* of the necessity of New Testament improvements in the matter of praise? Could it have been stronger *against* "the Psalms exclusively?" And the worst feature of the thing is, these children of the land of orthodoxy and Bible truth, though retaining the "paraphrase of Rouse," have repeated in the form of very *loose paraphrase*, one hundred and sixty-five selections from the old Psalms: for what purpose? Why do they give a second time these portions of the "inspired songs?" Why obliterate the *order* and connection in which the Holy Spirit placed them? Our exclusive brethren have an answer ready at hand—because, as we suppose, like the Old School church, these Scottish Presbyterians "*think they can write better than David!*" We are certainly found in excellent company. The exclusive principle, at least, hardly "finds rest for the sole of its foot" in the land of Knox, Hamilton, Chalmers, and others of the true Presbyterian nobility.

In this country, too, as early as 1787, in an extended "overture" prepared by a committee of the Associate Reformed General Synod, (at Philadelphia, May 16,) and consisting of Dr. John Mason, Robert Annan and John Smith, there occurred the following utterances on this subject: "We are extremely sorry to have observed a growing disrelish, in some churches, for the Psalms of David and *other songs of Scripture.* * * * And we do not mean to say, that *hymns of human composition* may not *be lawfully used* in any case whatever." This "overture" was written by Rev. R. Annan,* and we have personal knowledge that in his latter years he did not hold the exclusive views.

Twenty three years later (1810) the same Synod of the Associate Reformed church received "the report of a committee," in which they speak of the "very *critical condition* of a large section of their body, arising from the unpopularity of our present version (Rouse's) of the Psalms. * * From Washington northward," they say, "our present version is the *chief obstacle* to our prosperity, * * * and our social praise *languishes and is ready to die.* * * * Either the rising generation will take the reform into their own hands, and then there will be no computing the disasters of such a precedent; or our churches will be *swept entirely away.*" The remedy proposed by the committee, was "an improved version of scriptural Psalmody." Observe, they do not say, "an improved version of David's Psalms," but "of scriptural Psalmody"—probably designing to include the other songs and suitable parts of Scripture. These dissatisfactions have never entirely ceased in that denomination, and no doubt formed one of the reasons why so many of her ministers and members have sought refuge in the bosom of the Presbyterian church. There was no action

* This was the honored father of the writer—and as his name is often referred to in this controversy, we take pleasure in quoting from the Life of Dr. J. M. Mason the following extract from a letter by Dr. E. Dickey. He says, in referring to the proposed union between the Associate Reformed and the General Assembly: "It is the opinion of Mr. Annan, which he has openly expressed and frequently to me in private conversation, that such a thing (viz. the union) *ought to be brought about.*" This was as early as 1802. p. 420.

on the above report to the Synod, though the subject originated in a petition from *the people*, and was from highly respectable sources. It is well known, however, that some years later, the majority of the Associate Reformed Synod united with the Presbyterian body, thus fulfilling the *earnest desire* of one who has always been viewed as a chief instrument in originating the Associate Reformed church.

The history of our own times is equally instructive. In 1852 the late venerable Dr. M'Master published the fourth edition of his "Apology for the book of Psalms." He was an honored and influential minister of the Reformed Presbyterian body, or Covenanters. Though he and his brethren had, as a matter of expediency, prohibited by express rule the use in their churches of any but the "Psalms of David," he uttered at the close of his book, and near the close of his life, the following sentiments:—"If the church authorize it, collect from the books of inspiration *at large*, a volume or volumes of poetic matter, in prose or verse, leaving her ministers and people to use or not to use it."

Again, says Dr. M'Master, "When the sources of *inspired poetry* are exhausted * * * * let the church in council, endeavor to ascertain what may be necessary, safe, or advisable to do," &c. Dr. M'Master wished to retain a version of the Psalms, but had no objection to other songs of praise.

These are certainly liberal sentiments—worthy of the head and heart of their author. And we have reason to know that they still express the views of a large number, perhaps all, of the (New School) ministers and membership of that body. They show that the idea of the exclusive use of David's Psalms has but feeble hold upon the understanding and hearts of that respected denomination.

We are glad to be able to state further, that the discussions of some years past appear to have had a favorable influence upon the minds of prominent ministers of the

Associate Reformed church, now united with the Seceders. Some years ago, the two brethren of that body who have written most on the subject, assumed such positions as these—"It is the *will* of God that the songs contained in the book of Psalms be sung in his worship to the end of time, and we have *no authority* to use any other." * "And those who depart from this *appointment*, are seriously *corrupting* one of the most interesting and important ordinances of God." † But in subsequent publications the *tone* of these assumptions appears much subdued. We then are told that if the principle of *inspired Psalmody exclusively* be held, "the difference of opinion about the use of *any song* of praise contained in the Bible" is "not of such a nature as *should disturb* the peace of the church." ‡ Again, we are told, "the difference (between the churches of Scotland and the Associate Reformed church) is *comparatively small*, and would never in all probability have disturbed the peace of the church." || Thus observe the change of sentiment in a few years. In the former case it reads, the use of any but David's Psalms "*seriously corrupts* one of the most important ordinances of God;" but in the latter "*the difference is* SO SMALL AS NOT TO DISTURB THE PEACE OF THE CHURCH." We are happy to hail this shifting of original positions, and apparent movement toward the large scriptural ground of the Presbyterian church. § In fact our brother of the "Preacher" here gives up the chief debatable ground in regard to evangelical hymns of "human composition." The *five* such hymns, no less than the sixty-five "paraphrases" sung by the Free and Established churches of Scotland, are included in his

* Dr. Pressly, quoted by Ralston, p. 46.

† Preacher, by Dr. Kerr, June 9, 1847.

‡ Pressly on Psalmody, p. 88.

|| Preacher, by Dr. Kerr, September, 1852.

§ A writer in the Due West Telescope, the organ of the Associate Reformed Synod of the South, says (March, 1854): "*Nor do we object to versifying other portions of the Scriptures and using them in the worship of God.*"

admission as stated above. The *principle,* of course, is the same as though they were five or fifty times that number. Yet he says, "the difference is *comparatively small*"—"should not disturb the peace of the church." The first lines of these five Scottish hymns are as follows:

When all thy mercies, O my God!
The spacious firmament on high.
When rising from the bed of death.
Blessed morning! whose first dawning rays.
The hour of my departure 's come.

The first three are from the pen of Addison, and one of the others, we believe, from Dr. Watts. They are, in the broadest sense, "mere human compositions."

It would appear then from these concessions, that whilst one of these brethren will "*not disturb* the peace of the church" by opposing the use of any *song* of praise contained in the Bible;" the other, Rev. Dr. Kerr, editor of the "Preacher," goes much farther than "the *songs* of the Bible." He pleads for *peace* in regard to all such evangelical "human compositions" as the forementioned, by Addison and Dr. Watts. "*The difference,*" he says, "is comparatively small, and should not disturb the peace of the church." He will never quarrel with the Scottish churches for singing any such hymns of an evangelical character. They are *small* matters, not worth contending about over there in the land of Knox. But if this be so, why does he denounce these "human compositions" so bitterly, when they are found in our collection? We cannot *search the heart* for *all* the reasons which he and his brethren have for their great partiality toward hymn-singing Scotland. The avowed reason, however, we understand to be this, that we hymn-singing Americans "*impiously reject* the songs which God has given" and substitute Dr. Watts' productions in their place—or, in plainer language, we sing Watts' "paraphrase" instead of "Rouse's paraphrase." In other words, we Presbyterians treat "the Psalms" so badly, that the very hymns which are *quite tolerable* in Scotland, must *be resisted* on this side of the great water.

The *consistency* of this leniency toward Scottish hymns of "mere human composition," with other oft expressed sentiments of Dr. K. and his brethren, is a matter of minor concern. But from the foregoing induction, we feel authorized to put on distinct record the following propositions as conceded by these brethren, the first by Dr. P., the second by Dr. K., viz.:

I. The use in Divine worship of ANY SONG of praise contained in any part of the Bible, should not disturb the peace of the church, provided the principle of "inspired Psalmody" be preserved.

II. The use of HYMNS of *human composition*, in the circumstances of the Presbyterian churches of Scotland, should not disturb the peace of the church.

If, then, we have rightly understood the views of the brethren referred to, Dr. Pressly is ready to tolerate any of our hymns, provided it is "a song of the Holy Scriptures," and we hold his principle of "inspired Psalmody." And Dr. Kerr will not *disturb the peace* by warring against any of our hymns, even though it be like the hymns of the Free church of Scotland, "*mere human* composition," *provided* we consent to sing "Rouse's paraphrase" along with the hymns. These are legitimate and gratifying inferences from the doctrines avowed by these brethren. On the conditions stated, the difference becomes "comparatively small," and should make no disturbance in the church. We would thus place ourselves in the same position with the churches of Scotland, whose *hymns* of "mere human composure," according to Dr. Kerr, are quite tolerable, certainly not worth contending about! If we will only use Rouse or other "inspired Psalmody," our "hymns of human composition" will then become current with Dr. K. and his brethren equally with the "mere human effusions" of the churches of Scotland! We are glad to find that our brethren have become so very tolerant toward such "*serious corruptions* of Divine worship."

In the light of this brief history, we open the volume which contains the hymns used in the Old School Presbyterian church. And here the first thing that strikes us is, how large a proportion of these hymns are versified "songs of praise contained in the Bible." Of course, it follows, according to the judgment of one of these brethren, that "a difference of opinion" about the use of this whole class *should not disturb the peace of the church,* provided we will sing Rouse's paraphrase, or other equally inspired system. Take the very first hymn in the order of Dr. Watts. It is a paraphrase of Revelation 5 : 6–12. We have room for only a few verses:

And the four beasts and four and twenty elders fell down before the Lamb, having every one of them harps, golden vials full of odors.	Let elders worship at his feet, The church adore around, With vials full of odors sweet, And harps of sweeter sound.
And they sung a new song, * * Worthy is the Lamb that was slain to receive power, and riches, and wisdom, and strength, and honor, and glory, and blessing.	Now to the Lamb that once was slain, Be endless blessings paid; Salvation, glory, joy remain For ever on thy head.
Thou wast slain, and hast redeemed us to God by thy blood, &c.	Thou hast redeemed our souls with blood, Hast set the prisoners free, Hast made us kings and priests to God, And we shall reign with thee.

The first book of Dr. Watts contains one hundred and fifty of these paraphrases of Scripture, which to a very large extent are as near to the original text as many portions of the paraphrases of Rouse. They are not all "songs of praise," but many of them are, nor should they be allowed to "*disturb the peace of the church.*" In speaking of these paraphrases of his first book, Dr. Watts says, "I have borrowed *the sense* and much of the form of the song from *particular portions of Scripture,* and have paraphrased most of the doxologies in the New Testament and many parts of the Old Testament also, that have a reference to the times of the Messiah."

Of his second book of one hundred and seventy pieces, Dr. W. says, "I might have brought some text (of Scripture) and applied it to the margin of every verse, if this method had been as useful as it was easy." Still he candidly admits that the form of these hymns of book second, is of "mere human composure;" meaning that the *order* and *connection* of the song are not found in the Bible. Here, also, we have the judgment of Dr. K. in our favor. These hymns are, to say the very least, not more entirely "human compositions" than those adopted by the Free and Established churches of Scotland. Yet of these latter Dr. K. says, "their use in that country should not disturb the peace of the church." And by parity of reasoning in the Presbyterian church of this country, they ought not to be, on one condition, a source of contention or disturbance of the peace. At least *eleven* of these identical "human compositions" of Dr. Watts, are used by those Scottish churches, and Dr. K. assures us they "ought not to disturb the peace," provided Rouse be also used; or at least some equally inspired versification.

The same *toleration* is of course to be extended to the third book of Dr. Watts' hymns. It consists of forty-five pieces, of which the author says, "some are paraphrases of Scripture." They are intended especially to be used in the celebration of the Lord's Supper. Not a solitary hymn can be found in the whole three books, that is more really "a mere human composition" than a number of those in the Scottish collection, and which Dr. K. says furnish in Scotland no sufficient cause for contention or breach of the peace.

It appears, therefore, that the *casus belli*, the great source of the strife on the subject of Psalmody, according to Dr. K., is this : We Presbyterians "*impiously reject* the Psalms which God has given to be sung." But is this a correct statement? We deny it *in toto*, for the following reasons:

1. Our Supreme Judicatory has expressly *authorized* the Psalms in "Rouse's paraphrase" to be sung in all our churches. See the Act quoted in a former Letter. Is this the same as *impiously* rejecting them?

2. Our church, after careful revision and amendments made by the General Assembly, has also authorized the use of the Psalms in Dr. Watts' "paraphrase;" and besides, she has recently printed in connection with it, fifty selections from Rouse. Is this rejecting "the Psalms?"

3. All our churches are at perfect liberty to use one or the other of these versifications at their pleasure. If *every congregation* in our connection were immediately to *reject* every thing but Rouse, they would only do what they are authorized to do by our highest ecclesiastical court.

And now, in the name of peace, how is this the same as "*impiously rejecting* the Psalms?" True, our congregations generally, of the two authorized "paraphrases," prefer Watts to Rouse—but even if the General Assembly, instead of authorizing had expressly *forbidden* Rouse's paraphrase, can any person really persuade himself that this would be the same as "*impiously* rejecting the Psalms which God has given?" But they have not forbidden even that paraphrase, but given it their sanction.

The same reasoning applies to all the other hymns in the Presbyterian collection, which are by other authors than Dr. W. The great mass of the verses are merely expanded texts of God's blessed Word. For example, Hymn 232:

Stretched on the cross the Saviour dies,	Matthew 27: 35.
Hark! his expiring groans arise;	Matthew 27: 46.
See how the sacred crimson tide	Hebrews 9: 14.
Flows from his hands, his feet, his side.	John 19: 34.

Whether such compositions as this deserve to be

stigmatized as "mere human inventions," is a question not difficult to decide.

We have already shown that there is not a solitary instance in the New Testament of a Psalm of David being sung. On the contrary, the apostles and brethren used the book of Psalms in quite another manner, in the *two examples* in which alone they appear to have employed them in social praise. The first case is Luke 19 : 38. The disciples assumed part of a verse from Psalm 118, but sung it with alterations to adapt it to their circumstances. The other example is in Acts 4 : 24, where the beginning of the 2d Psalm is sung by Peter, John, and their company. You find there an addition of praise in the beginning—then a narration of what David spoke—then an application to Herod, Pontius Pilate, &c.—then they enlarge the matter of fact by considering the hand of God in it, and the song concludes with the breathing of their desires toward God for mercies most precisely suited to their day and duty; and having sung, they went to prayer, and then preached with amazing success.

We have here an *inspired* example of that identical use of the Psalms and of *other inspired matter*, which our church sanctions. It is an apostolic hymn, which nowhere appears in David, and affords abundant warrant from "the Author of light and wisdom" for the hymns of the Presbyterian church. The apostles seem to have known nothing of the "Divine appointment" of "the sweet Psalmist of Israel," to that exclusive authority for the church in all ages.

This apostolic example of grouping together parts of the Psalms with other inspired matter, is the very *principle* on which most of our hymns are arranged. Our brethren practice the same thing in preaching the gospel, expounding the Scriptures, "*explaining* the Psalms," and in prayer. It is by their own admission, perfectly right in every other part of worship. How, then, does it become a *daring impiety* in the matter of praise? How can the addition *of a tune* to a brief "explanation" of a Psalm, render it a solemn mockery of God?

In strong corroboration of these views, the visions of the book of Revelation distinctly point out the very style, sentiment and manner of the *praises* of the New Testament church. Take for example, Revelation 5: 9–14. Our soundest commentators inform us that John's visions in "heaven" shadowed forth the visible church on earth. Thus Dr. Scott, "These adoring praises were rendered by the *representatives* of the church." "Thus the whole church, by its representatives, fell down and worshiped." "These (especially the four and twenty elders) are *generally allowed* to be the emblematic representatives of the whole church of God." They were engaged in worshiping God and the Lamb. What do they sing? A Psalm of David? No such thing. "WORTHY IS THE LAMB THAT WAS SLAIN." See the whole hymn in Revelation 5: 9–14. Several similar songs are found in the same book. If there were no other evidence in favor of our New Testament hymns, this would be conclusive. We cannot be wrong in singing the very hymns which the Spirit of prophecy dictated to "the beloved disciple," as the subject matter of the exalted praises of God's people in all future ages; and especially since these hymns were communicated as the very essence and joy of the worship that employs the blest voices of redeemed spirits in the presence of God.* Men may denounce such songs as "corruptions," but they are not so esteemed in the world of glory.

* "Though *heaven* is the scene of these visions, yet * * * * * *the state of the church on earth* is throughout particularly adverted to." —*Scott.*

LETTER XII.

EARLY USE OF HYMNS IN THE CHURCH — GLANCE AT EPHES. 5 : 19; COLOS. 3 : 16 — AUTHORITY OF RALPH ERSKINE IN FAVOR OF OUR INTERPRETATION — PRIMITIVE CHURCH, HER USAGE — OBJECTIONS ANSWERED: "BOOK OF PSALMS PERFECT"—"NO COMMAND TO MAKE SONGS OF PRAISE"—"SETTING ASIDE PARTS OF GOD'S WORD"—"LEADS TO ALTERATION OF THE INSPIRED RECORD"—"HYMNS ENCOURAGE ERROR AND HERESY"—"LEADS TO SCHISM AND DISCORD," &C.

MY DEAR SIR:—The history of the early use of hymns, viz. songs of praise not found in the book of Psalms, affords some instructive lessons.

Even in the inspired record of the life of Jesus, we find the author of the gospel by Mark employing a Greek word to express the singing of the Saviour and his disciples at the Passover and the Lord's Supper, which word, *humnesantes*, or *having hymned* or "*sung a hymn*," is not the common one to indicate the Psalms. In every place but one in the New Testament which refers *beyond all doubt* to "David's Psalms," the word is *psalmos*, not *humnos*, or the corresponding verb. If, as is strenuously maintained by our brethren, the Saviour selected Psalms 113–118 for this hymn, * it would have been more natural for Mark to employ the usual term to indicate that the Psalms were sung. We admit, however, that Josephus, the Jewish historian, applies the terms "hymns and songs" to the Bible Psalms. Antiquities 7 : 12, 3. And it is said that the Jews at the time of the Advent of Christ, were accustomed to sing the great Hallel (Psalms 113–118,) at the celebration of the Passover. If this were so, it was an *innovation* on the original appointment, which does not include singing. See the record, Exodus 12 : 1–28. Besides, the Hallel (or Psalms 113–

* The Jews of that period, it is said, sung Psalms 113 and 114 before the Passover, and the others (115–118) after it.

118,) was not composed for several hundred years afterward.

The question, however, whether the Lord Jesus sung a part of the book of Psalms in connection with the Passover, is of very small importance in this discussion. Admitting that he sung the Hallel—then if we were required to observe the Jewish Passover, we should feel bound to copy his example, even in this particular, (as in circumcision,) in order, like him, "to fulfill all righteousness." But how does such an example decide *for* or *against* the dogma, which affirms the Hebrew Psalm book to be the *only and universal Psalmody* of all ages? If Christ and his disciples sung a part of the Psalms, they did only what every sound Presbyterian joyfully and thankfully approves and copies — a privilege which he very highly appreciates. But to sing any other portion of the holy oracles—is that the same as "offering strange fire?" There is the true point in debate.

The term *humnos*, hymn, is found only twice in the New Testament, viz. in those well contested passages, Ephesians 5 : 19, and Colossians 3 : 16 : "Speaking to yourselves in Psalms, hymns, *humnois*, and spiritual songs." It suits the exclusive theory of our brethren, to affirm that these three terms in both passages, "probably indicate sacred songs which *are substantially the same*;"* that is, they all mean the Psalms of David. But here the best authorities are against them. Henry says: "By Psalms may be meant David's Psalms, or such composures as were fitly sung with musical instruments. By *hymns*, such others as were confined to matter of praise, as those of Zacharias, Simeon," &c. Doddridge adds: "I see not the authority for supposing all these words to refer to David's poetical pieces," &c.† Dr. Scott says the words mean, "the Psalms and hymns of the *sacred Scriptures* and such spiritual songs as *pious men composed* on the peculiar subjects of the gospel."

* Pressly on Psalmody, p. 140.

† See also Macknight on the Epistles.

Again, he interprets these words to mean, "hymns and songs of praise to God, and *poems of every kind* which are suited to prepare them for the worship of heaven: and let them use these hymns and songs *constantly*, not on public occasions alone, but in social meetings also," &c. The learned editor of the Comprehensive Commentary, Dr. Jenks, says: "*Psalmoi*, not simply David's, for then the article would have been used, *hoi Psalmoi*. The words certainly comprehended other compositions." Dr. Hodge, in his Commentary on Ephesians, takes the same large view, and adds as one of the scriptural meanings of *psalmos*, Psalm: "Any sacred poem formed on the Old Testament Psalms, as in 1 Corinthians 14 : 26, where *psalmon* appears to mean such *a song given by inspiration*, and not one of the Psalms of David." Such is the unanimous testimony of these commentators: they are in direct opposition to the view held by these brethren, viz. that by "Psalms, hymns and songs," Paul meant exclusively the book of Psalms.

But it is replied that the churches of Ephesus and Colosse had in their possession the Psalms of David, and they had no other—therefore they would most certainly understand the apostle as referring to the book of Psalms alone. But it seems to be forgotten that those churches were recently formed amid a heathen population and in heathen cities — books were scarce, and having to be copied by the hand on wax, lead, parchment or similar materials, were extremely expensive; and the ability to read was by no means general. Besides, when the apostle rebukes the Corinthians as follows: "Every one of you hath a Psalm"—the common interpretation is, that these *Psalms* were the fruits of the gifts of the Holy Spirit then bestowed upon the membership of the Corinthian church.* Then why might not the same Divine influence have been found at Ephesus and Colosse? And why may not Paul refer to this class of Psalms, as

* See Prof. Hodge's Commentary on Ephesians; also various other commentators of the best repute.

well as to those of David? In view of the whole argument, it appears *most evident*, as Dr. Hodge remarks, "that not only Psalms, but *hymns* as distinct compositions, also were employed." As to the Septuagint use of the term, when Isaiah would predict the glorious triumphs of the gospel, he exclaims—"Sing unto the Lord a new song (*humnon* or hymn), and his praise from the ends of the earth." Chapter 42 : 10. The Greek is very expressive—"*Hymn* unto the Lord a *new hymn*." The hymn immediately follows, and though not found in "the book of Psalms," Isaiah exhorts to sing it, including, of course, all similar hymns; an exhortation or command just as binding upon the New Testament church as any requirement to "sing Psalms" which is found in the book of that name.

But in ascertaining the correct meaning of these two celebrated texts, (Ephesians 5 : 19; Colossians 3 : 16,) we have decidedly in our favor no less a personage than the distinguished patriarch of the Associate or Seceder Presbytery of Scotland, RALPH ERSKINE. This may seem strange, but it is not the less true. In the preface to his poetical "paraphrase" upon the "Song of Solomon," after speaking of the "Song" as full of Christ, he says: "I judge that *a song upon this subject* is not unseasonable, when the songs of the temple (the church) are like to be turned into howlings, &c. How desirable," he adds, "that this little book might help her to *sing away* her sorrows, * * to drive away the night of trouble *with songs* of praise," &c. "WE HAVE A DIVINE PRECEPT," he continues, "perhaps too much forgotten and neglected, in Ephesians 5 : 18, 19, and Colossians 3 : 16." "Likewise an express Divine appointment in Psalm 46 : 6, 7, how we are to sing," &c. "Now this sacred Song of Solomon being very mysterious, that you may be the more *able to sing it* over with understanding, I have endeavored to lay open the mysteries," &c. He then states that he "had cast his paraphrase in the mould of common metre" for the purpose of singing.

Here, then, it will be seen that Ralph Erskine interprets Paul's "Psalms, hymns and spiritual songs," as A DIVINE PRECEPT *to sing* the "Song of Solomon." And his recommendation of the "Song" is not only for private devotion, but as he says, "*to help her* (the church) to *sing away her sorrows* with these songs of praise." Surely Ralph Erskine had not before his eyes the fear of "the sin of Nadab and Abihu!" The truth is, he had no dogma of *exclusive* Psalmody to warp his judgment, and therefore he uttered the sentiments of piety and good sense. It is certainly worthy of distinct record, that a man "whose name," as Dr. Beveridge affirms, "deserves to be held in everlasting remembrance," should have thus discovered in these oft disputed texts, "*a Divine precept*" to sing other productions than the one hundred and fifty Psalms—and that, too, at the very period when, as he says, "the songs of the church (Rouse) were turned into howlings!"

But perhaps it will be replied, that Erskine refers only to an "inspired song," and therefore, he does not approve "human composition." But this is a mistake. He calls his poetical work, "a paraphrase, or large explicatory poem." The first line of the "Song," viz. its naked *title*, he expands into four stanzas of four lines each, and so of the rest. The line, verse 4, "Draw me; we will run after thee" — is paraphrased into twelve lines. Erskine's paraphrase is no more an inspired song than the "*explanation of the Psalm*" by the Associate Reformed minister. Yet this distinguished father and founder of the Associate or Seceder body, finds "A DIVINE PRECEPT" for singing this "human production" in the words of Paul, Ephesians 5 : 18, 19, and Colossians 3 : 16. Thus the evidence is full and clear, that the interpretation which makes "Psalms, hymns and spiritual songs" to refer exclusively to the Psalms of David, is a *novelty* got up to suit a particular purpose. "*The wish* is the father of the thought."

That the primitive church, i. e., the church in the ages

immediately succeeding the apostles, was not restricted tc the book of Psalms as their only Psalmody, is so clearly demonstrated by history as to admit of no doubt. Thus the celebrated Neander writes as follows: "*Singing* also passed from the Jewish service into that of the Christian church. St. Paul exhorts the early Christians to sing spiritual songs. What was used for this purpose were partly the Psalms of the Old Testament, and partly *songs composed with this very object:* especially songs of praise and thanks to God and Christ, and these we know Pliny found to be customary among the Christians. In the controversies with the Unitarians, about the end of the second century, and the beginning of the third, the hymns in which, from early times, Christ had been honored as God, were appealed to."

This is clear and decisive:

1. The praises of the church were offered *in part,* in the language of the Psalms of David.

2. They were offered also in songs (or hymns) composed with this very object.

3. These songs of praise to God and Christ, were afterward quoted, in controversy with Unitarians. The Christians of the close of the second and beginning of the third centuries, cited them as hymns to Christ as God, and as the testimony of "early times to his divinity." It is true, the learned Spanheim takes a different view. He says, in speaking of the fourth century: "That besides *hymns* and *songs* and private *Psalms,* of which there was a great number in their solemn assemblies, the *Psalm book* of David was brought into the western church in this age."

With this testimony agrees that of the learned and generally accurate Mosheim. In his account of the worship of the fourth century, he says: "The Psalms of David were now received among the public hymns that were sung as a part of Divine service." For his authority, Mosheim refers to Cyril of Jerusalem, the apostolical constitutions, and Beausobre.

The difference between these profound historians, it will be observed, is not as to "*other productions*" being sung—in this they agree. The *only point* of dispute is, *whether the Psalms of David were used in public praise prior to* the fourth century. Neander, and more recently Schaff of this country, are of opinion that portions of those Psalms were sung in the churches from the beginning. Spanheim and Mosheim decide, "*not until the fourth century.*" For some further references the reader may see Letter XIV.

We do not deem it at all necessary to examine minutely certain historical citations made by the friends of Rouse. Admitting the correctness of the quotations from early writers, as they are adduced by our brethren — what would they prove? Only this — that portions of "the book of Psalms" were employed in praising God. But no sound Presbyterian regards this as a fact of any importance in this discussion. We rather rejoice to know that it was so. We practice the same thing. It is the custom among our churches to sing parts of "the Psalms of David" every Lord's day, as we think it highly probable the early Christians did. But here is the point to be settled — "Did any one of those primitive Christians regard the book of Psalms as the *only, universal and perpetual* Psalmody of the church for all ages?" Did any one of them ever *dream* that it was a *high crime,* scarcely less heinous than that of Uzza, Nadab, Abihu, &c., to worship God in *any other songs* of praise? Let them produce a solitary *scrap* from any writer of those early times to prove these points, and then we will attend to their demonstrations. Till then, we will continue to believe that the primitive church found "A DIVINE PRECEPT," as Ralph Erskine did, (in Ephesians 5 : 19 ; Colossians 3 : 26,) for singing *human paraphrases* of the "Song of Solomon," as well as all other suitable portions of the Scriptures. And further, that many of those primitive Christians were highly gifted by the Father of lights, to enable them to compose suitable songs of praise. As a specimen, Basil, of the fourth century, cites one that had become *very ancient* even in his day, and which is translated by Dr. Pye Smith as follows: "Jesus Christ — joyful Light of the Holy! Glory of the Eternal, heavenly, holy, blessed Father! Having now come to the setting of the sun—beholding the evening light, we praise the Father and the Son and the Holy Spirit of God. Thou art worthy to be praised of sacred voices, at all seasons, O Son of God, who givest life. Wherefore the universe glorifieth Thee!"

Another, equally ancient, begins thus: "We praise thee—we sing hymns to thee—we bless thee—we glorify thee—we worship thee—by thy great High Priest; thou who art the true God—who art the One unbegotten," &c. In such strains the early Christians conducted the service of song.

It was of such hymns as these Clemens of Alexandria (about A. D. 175,) wrote as follows: "Gather together thy children to praise the Leader of children, the eternal *Logos*, the eternal Light, the Fountain of mercy. Filled with the dew of the Spirit, let us sing sincere praises, genuine hymns to Christ our king." *

From the fourth century down to the period of the glorious Reformation, no one can question the common use of hymns not found among the one hundred and fifty Psalms. The martyrs, Huss and Jerome, who were burned by the Papists at the Council of Constance, sung such hymns, even amid their last sufferings. Of Jerome, history says: "As he went to execution he sung the Apostles' creed and the hymns of the church with a loud voice and a cheerful countenance. He kneeled at the stake and prayed. Being then bound he raised his voice and sung a paschal hymn, then much in vogue in the church:

'Hail! happy day, and ever be adored,
When hell was conquered by great heaven's Lord.'"

Luther wrote many hymns, among others a small vol-

* For some further proofs and examples of these primitive hymns, see Letter No. XIV.

ume of about forty pieces, for the celebration of the Lord's Supper. Nor was there in that noble offshoot of the Reformation, the church of Scotland, any great hostility to hymns. To the copies which we have seen of her earliest paraphrase of the Psalms, Sternhold and Hopkins, we find prefixed *thirteen* hymns, including the songs of Zacharias and Mary. *Twelve* similar songs stand at the close, including "songs to be sung before morning and evening prayer"—"a prayer to be sung before the sermon," and "a thanksgiving after receiving the Lord's Supper." Here are twenty-five hymns attached to the Psalms of David, and bound with the Bible! Can any one doubt with what object? These songs are for the most part not even paraphrases of portions of Scripture, but "mere human compositions." To what extent they were used, we have no means of information. Such a *prefix* or *appendix* to *Rouse*, in these modern times, would produce some astonishment, if tolerated and published by our strict brethren in this country.

Let us now turn to some of *the objections* to our views:

1. "The book of Psalms is an inspired system of Psalmody." "It is the workmanship of God; * * it is perfect, and as a system needs no addition."*

But it has been shown in previous Letters, that it was not so viewed even by the Jews. Hezekiah, the mourners for Josiah, &c., used "other productions."

Again: We admit that for all the purposes for which *it was designed*, as "the production of Infinite Wisdom," as a precious part of "the rule of faith," &c., the book of Psalms is "*perfect.*" But David in the 19th Psalm says, "The law of the Lord is *perfect.*" What did he mean? Doubtless God's holy Word. And how large a part, even of the Old Testament, did the church possess at that period? Certainly, the five books of Moses, and perhaps the other historical records of Samuel and the Kings, and some of the Psalms. If the law of the Lord was *perfect* then, (to say nothing of the New Testament,)

* Pressly on Psalmody, pp. 142, 189.

where was the use of those Psalms which were not composed at that period, and of the prophets who lived in subsequent ages? We hold the *perfection* of the Psalms, just as we hold the perfection of the "law," viz. a *perfection* which admits all the clearer Divine revelations of subsequent periods—a perfection for *the uses* for which it *was designed* by Infinite Wisdom. Let it be proved that God designed the book of Psalms as a perfect and all-sufficient system of praise for all ages, and the *objection* will then cease to be a mere *begging of the question.*

2. Another objection: "In the book of Psalms, not an attribute of the Deity, not a *work that he has done,* but here stands forth in bold relief."* If this were true, it would render almost useless all the rest of the inspired volume. What more do we want than all the attributes of God, and all his *works* of creation, providence and redemption? But where in the Psalms are we told that Christ should appear in this world as a *little child,* "the babe of Bethlehem," not as a full grown and perfect man? Where do they teach that he should be born of a virgin—that Mary of Nazareth was to be his mother—and that "Jesus of Nazareth" was the long-predicted Messiah, to the exclusion of all "false Christs?" Where are we told of that most affecting *work* of mercy, the pardon of the thief on the cross? Where, the institution of the Lord's Supper, and the change of the Sabbath from the seventh to the first day of the week? "*Not a work* that *he has done!*" Was the Reformation under Luther "a work of God?" What Psalm speaks of it? And so we might run on for pages, exposing the folly of those who claim for the "book of Psalms" a *perfection* which its glorious Author never designed it should possess.† In their zeal for a denominational dogma, these

* Preacher, Dec. 29, 1858.

† "If you want a book which shall adequately set forth the high praises of the Lord our God, *for all he is and for all he has done,* in the vast ranges of *creation, providence and redemption,* then we need no other, and can find no other than this book."—*United Presbyterian,* of Cincinnati.

brethren seem to forget that "life and immortality are *brought to light* in the gospel."

3. Third objection. "We have no command to *make* songs of praise, in addition to those composed by David and the others in the book of Psalms." Neither is there any command to *make* sermons. We have the precept, "Preach the word," which implies that our discourses must be composed. So we have a command to sing praises, and the inspired hymns and examples of those who composed *other songs* than are found among the one hundred and fifty Psalms. Will it be said, that God has not given us a "book of sermons," but has given us a "book of Psalms?" This is a mistake. The title of "the book of Ecclesiastes," not only in the original Hebrew, but in the Septuagint, Vulgate and English versions, is "the Preacher." Here are the *dibrai koheleth*, "the words of the Preacher," his public discourses, or a collection of *inspired sermons*. Besides, what forms the greater part of the prophets, to say nothing of the public addresses of Moses, and Solomon, and Ezra, and Nehemiah, and Job? Are there not in the New Testament, also, a large number of the discourses of the Saviour and his Apostles? The whole Bible is, in great part, a collection of "inspired sermons." Well, then, as there is no divine precept to *make* sermons, why does the preacher presume to compose them? Does he think he can make *better* discourses than inspired men, yea, than even the Divine Saviour himself! So it would seem; otherwise he would use those already prepared, *perfect* sermons, "the workmanship of God, productions of Infinite Wisdom." What *profane* men these preachers must be, thus "*impiously* to *reject*" the discourses God has composed, and inspired prophets and apostles preached, in order to give a *preference* to their own effusions!* The same reasoning holds good in regard to the

* We admit that the apostles composed sermons—but they were inspired men—and it remains to be proved that their example authorizes every preacher to prefer "his own effusions."

"human composition" of their prayers, in preference to the very numerous prayers composed by inspired men.

4. These brethren object to our theory as involving the profane idea that "some parts of the word of God may be laid aside as useless, while other portions may be selected and profitably retained."* This has been already answered. Do not these objectors, to a much larger extent, *lay aside* many parts of the discourses of the Bible? Did they ever preach one of them in place of one of their own? Thus they "entirely omit many whole sermons, and large pieces of many others!" The very thing which they charge upon Dr. Watts "as a contempt of the Spirit of Inspiration," they themselves practice in their discourses and in their public prayers! They group together texts from all quarters, from Genesis to Revelation, and *thus patch* up their own "human compositions," which they exalt above the word of God, viz., by setting aside "inspired sermons" to make room for their own productions. Besides, are there no parts of the word of God which these brethren "*lay aside as useless*" for the public reading of the Scriptures? Does Dr. P. ever read from the pulpit certain passages in the Levitical law? Does he ever quote such texts in the presence of his congregation? No, he purposely avoids them. See, then, how he "*lays aside* some parts of the Holy Scripture as useless" in public worship! Of course, it follows that he must think "the word of God given in a very defective form!" Thus he decides that certain portions of Divine truth are unsuitable for public worship! How shocking!

5. It is objected, that our method of employing the book of Psalms in praise, involves as a legitimate result, that men may alter and improve the whole Bible, the rule of faith, &c. And it gives a license, it is said, to every "imitator and hymnographer to attempt to compose hymns to thrust out the songs of Zion."

The answer is obvious: We believe "the whole word of God is of use to direct us in praise;" and that in the

* Pressly on Psalmody, p. 112.

whole ordering of the matter of *versions*, &c., *it is the duty of the church in her highest judicatory*, not of "*every imitator and hymnographer*," to take the exclusive direction. In this as in every other appropriate sphere of her duty, the church *has the promised presence and blessing of her Divine Master*, "Lo I am with you always, even to the end of the world; and where two or three are gathered in my name, there am I," &c.; and has a most clear and express title to expect the *aids of the Holy Spirit, certainly to say the least, with no less confidence than any individual minister is entitled to expect the aids of the Spirit in "the human composition" of his prayers!* If it be said that this is a very large and dangerous power to intrust in the hands of the church; we reply, not a whit larger or more dangerous than the *preparation of her Creed and Catechisms!* Not a whit larger or more dangerous than to intrust to the pastors of the church the *whole exposition* of the word of God, and especially *the whole explaining of the Psalms before they are sung*, thus "giving the gospel sense" to all that is typical, clearing up what is obscure, and instructing the people *in the doctrines* implied or expressed! Certainly the collective wisdom of the church may be as safely trusted, as these individual pastors.

We maintain that as the "rule of faith," the Bible cannot be altered for the better, either in whole or in part. But every preacher alters *the order and connection* of the Scriptures, both in his sermons and prayers. Why? To make them more plain and instructive to the people, and render the worship more impressive and useful.

Just so is it with the church in the *proper use* of the Psalms and other parts of Scripture for purposes of praise. There is no more attempt to be "wiser than God" in the latter case than in the former. Even Prof. Patterson decides that "the Psalms *need* exposition to open these sacred fountains, which otherwise remain sealed," &c. It *must be done* either in prose or verse—

either by the individual preacher in the pulpit, or under the supervision of the whole church in her highest court. Which is likely to be the *safer* guide, let common sense decide.

For such ends as these, it is obvious that in order to worship with "the spirit and the understanding also," adaptation is needful, yea indispensable; *selection* is lawful, *explanation* is absolutely necessary, transposition and grouping of parts may be highly expedient and proper, expounding typical matters, &c., may be highly commendable, condensation (as in creeds and catechisms) is the proper work of the church, &c. But surely it does not follow, because we advocate such liberties as these, that we must therefore to be consistent, attempt to amend "the rule of faith," "raise a hue and cry against the old Bible," &c. By no means. "The old Bible" is just what it ought to be, "the perfect Law of God." All that we teach is, that in the three great elements of public worship, preaching, prayer and praise, the church is entitled, yea, is bound in fidelity to her Divine Master, to use all the means and advantages which God has given her, to open and expound his Divine word, to employ its precious truths in the most suitable and edifying mode, and to draw from its inexhaustible stores, whether in the New Testament or the Old, the sacred and soul stirring themes, the blessed and delightful meditations, *the glorious truths and bright manifestations of God in the flesh*, the devout aspirations, &c., which have thrilled the hearts of God's children, both under the new and old dispensation, and formed the songs of angels and spirits of the just in heaven.

The sum of the argument is therefore briefly this: The "principles" on which the Presbyterian system of Psalmody is formed, are substantially the same as those on which all exposition, especially all lecturing upon select passages of Scripture, is conducted—the "principles" on which ministers compose their prayers and "*explain the Psalms*"—the "principles" on which the church assumes the immense responsibility of constructing her Creed and Catechisms; in a word, the same "principles" by which the church, as all admit, assumes the control and direction, under responsibility to her God, of every *other part* of Divine worship.

6. But it is alleged "that the tendencies of our hymns are strongly toward error and heresy—while the Psalms, wherever exclusively used, have proved highly conservative in keeping the church right."

But here the facts are generally the other way. Take the example of the Jews. They sung, they still sing, David's Psalms alone and in the original Hebrew. Have they always been remarkably free from idolatry, heresy and apostasy?

The blessed Saviour, too, a Divine Pastor, had a small congregation, which these brethren say praised God only in David. Were they, including the traitor Judas, all remarkable for stability in maintaining the truth? On a certain occasion "they ALL FORSOOK HIM AND FLED!"

The apostolic church, too, these brethren affirm, used only David. But how early did "the mystery of iniquity begin to work?" How soon were even apostles summoned to contend with deadly heresies and apostasies in the bosom of the churches they had planted? Singing the Psalms of David, even in their purest and most unadulterated form, was not a preventive of error among them, as their experience sadly testified. The Jews of the present day sing the Psalms of David in a much purer state than the friends of Rouse. The Arians of Ulster use the veritable "Old Rouse." They used it at the very time when their apostasy occurred. Perhaps, they also sung other productions; but in this they did nothing worse than the Free church of Scotland; nor is there the smallest evidence that to this source must be traced the apostasy of Ulster, any more than their volume of hymns by Watts and others, is likely to corrupt the Free church.

Again, all Protestant churches use the same Bible.

Then how absurd for any one to ascribe to any English versification, say the patchwork verse of Rouse, a higher usefulness and efficiency in any particular, than he ascribes to the pure word of God, including the Psalms in prose, and the New Testament.

7. The use of hymns, it is further objected, "promotes disunion and schism, while the tendencies of David exclusively are manifest toward union and harmony."

This is, perhaps, the most extraordinary of all objections. There are not less than five or six denominations which sing "Rouse's paraphrase?" They are quite small in numbers, and their differences are admitted to be of no very great magnitude. For many years two of the more harmonious among them have been holding conventions, composing platforms, issuing "Testimonies" and other bonds of union; writing, speaking, praying, preaching, yea, even *singing Rouse,* in order to promote their union. What has been the result? Why, instead of two sects, as formerly, there are now *three* composed of the same materials? Yet their leading authors bitterly reproach our *hymns* as sources of *division,* "sectarianism," &c.

Were all these smaller sects put together, they would not compose a body at all unwieldly for its magnitude—probably not over seven hundred or eight hundred ministers and perhaps seventy-five thousand communicants. Does this look like union and harmony? The "sectarian hymns" are not responsible for these divisions. They have all enjoyed an "inspired Psalmody"—but strange to say, it has neither prevented nor healed their fragmentary divisions and subdivisions, but a new one has just been added to the number.

Admitting that each denomination naturally wishes to have its Psalmody in concord with its doctrinal and practical views—and this is a result of common sense—what follows? Is it any better among those churches which sing Rouse? The plain truth is, that by "explaining the Psalm," these brethren make Rouse teach whatever *opinions* or "sectarian views" they may individually have adopted, just as the Arians of Ulster do—and what more can be said of the authorized Psalmody of all other denominations? Of course each sect will reflect its own views of Scripture in its preaching, its prayers, and its public praise, and there seems to be no cure for the evils of one, more than the evils of the others. Indeed, *preaching* error is a far more "powerful and certain agency for the increase and perpetuity of sectarianism," than praise.

Nor is the influence of Rouse in the Presbyterian churches of Scotland much better. The four principal denominations embrace a little over two thousand eight hundred congregations—being five hundred congregations less than belong to the Old School Presbyterians of this country. Has the Psalmody of Rouse always secured purity and concord there? Read Hetherington's history of "Moderatism," Burgher and Anti-Burgher strifes, &c. Read Dr. Beveridge's account * of the fearful conflicts in the days of the Erskines, when as Ralph says, "the *songs* of the temple were like to be turned into *howlings!*" Yes, even the "songs" of the anti-sectarian Rouse swept away by the flood of cold hearted "Moderatism," or turned into "*howlings!*" And as a remedy for these evils, Ralph Erskine recommends the singing of "Solomon's Song," &c.

But perhaps some one will now inquire—"Did ever any person of intelligence really make such an *objection* to the Presbyterian Psalmody?" We reply in two or three extracts from leading periodicals of our brethren: "These man-made books," they say, "are all and always *sectarian*, and their tendency is to perpetuate errors and divisions forever." "We have a Methodist hymn book, a Baptist hymn book, a Mormon hymn book, a Unitarian hymn book," &c. † Well, there would be some force in this, if the objector could persuade these several sorts of

* Church Memorial, pp. 18–25.

† United Presbyterian, of Cincinnati.

errorists to do all their *preaching and praying* according to Rouse, *as well as their singing*. And especially if he could persuade them to lay aside the time-honored custom of "explaining the Psalm!" But until this is done, we greatly fear the Mormons, not *unlike the Jews*, might sing even Rouse and be no nearer the true religion; and the Unitarian preacher, like *the Arian of Ulster*, might also sing Rouse; but by "*explaining the Psalms*," he would "wrest them, as he does the other Scriptures, to his own and his hearers destruction!" But of one thing we are perfectly sure—that by the singing of *the words* of Rouse with a Mormon or Socinian "explanation," no *great* advance would be made toward *union* and *harmony* among Christian churches!

But hear another defender of this sort of faith. In speaking of those who, as he alleges, "*set aside* the Divine system of praise," he says: "What is the spectacle which they present? The Calvinist praising the perfections and works of God as they appear in his system of theology; *the Arminian as they appear* in his; *the Universalist* as they appear in his; and so, down through every grade of error, from that which is nearest the truth to that which is most remote — making the worship of God as the confusion of Babel!" *

We greatly marvel that these brethren have entirely overlooked the Jews, and "the Arians of Ulster," especially the latter, in their anti-sectarian labors. Those respectable bodies certainly call for their sympathy as loudly, to say the very least, as the Mormons and Universalists. Particularly since they are so very anxious to effect a reform in what Dr. K. calls "THE WORSHIP OF GOD!"

But seriously—can any well informed person imagine that the Jew is less of a Jew, "the Arian of Ulster" less of an Arian—or either Arian or Jew less of *a sectary*, because they both sing "the Psalms," either in Rouse or in Hebrew? Or that any other sect, Mormon,

* Rev. Dr. Kerr, in Preacher, June 9, 1847.

Universalist, &c., would be at all nearer the Scriptural *oneness* of which Christ speaks, by singing Rouse as *explained* by their sectarian teachers! All Christian churches are instructed by their faithful pastors, to read and study diligently both the Testaments, including the book of Psalms. Still these studies do not lead them to the same precise conclusions in all minute matters of faith and practice. Nor can we reasonably expect any different result from their *singing* these Scriptures, or *any part* of them. Yet charity bids us entertain the belief that the leading denominations are ONE in "holding the Head." But what sort of *Christian union* would that be, even supposing all the sects to sing Rouse, if they still continued to teach and defend as earnestly as ever their several peculiarities? We have a *precious* example of this sort of *oneness* in the half dozen or more small bodies which agree in singing Rouse. *

We maintain that there is quite as much true Christian union in the vast majority of the evangelical world who reject Rouse, as among the small minority who use that Psalmody. The former can at least unite in the sweet anthem commencing:

All hail, the power of Jesus' name!
Let saints before him fall;
Bring forth the royal diadem,
And crown Him LORD of all.

And the same sweet harmony pervades the entire volume of their sacred songs, with comparatively few exceptions—*so few* as by no means to render their public praise "the Babel of confusion." Certainly not as much so as their public *prayer* and *preaching*. Does Dr. K. hold that the whole devotional services of the sanctuary as maintained by all Christian denominations, *except the few advocates*

* If *reading* in Divine worship the same prose version of the Bible, including the Psalms and the New Testament, does not produce harmony, how ridiculous to expect such a result from the addition of a *tune* to a part of the same inspired record; and much more to expect such a result from "old Rouse," with his four hundred or five hundred "human inventions."

of Rouse, are "the confusion of Babel?" So it would seem. Such are his "brotherly kindness and charity." We are suspicious of a zeal for union which brings forth such fruits. But enough of such remedies for *sectarism*. The men who can have faith in them, need not find it hard to believe that baptism is regeneration, or that prayer and praise are appreciated in heaven by the character of the *sound* rather than by the *sense*, by the words uttered with the lips, rather than by the spiritual emotions of the heart.

But why should the various Christian denominations differ on this subject — why not all agree to adopt "the Psalms" as their system of praise, and in "a literal and correct version?" This inquiry has been variously answered in our previous pages—but some further remarks will be given in our next Letter.

LETTER XIII.

BOOK OF PSALMS NOT DESIGNED TO BE THE ONLY AND PERPETUAL PSALMODY OF THE CHURCH — FIVE FURTHER ARGUMENTS TO PROVE IT — FRUITS OF THE EXCLUSIVE SYSTEM — SUSPENSION OF MINISTERS, ELDERS AND CHURCH MEMBERS—ARGUMENT FROM ANALOGY—PRAYER AND PRAISE — BOTH HUMAN COMPOSITION — SO MINGLED IN THE PSALMS AS TO BE INSEPARABLE, HENCE INCONSISTENCIES — STRANGE JARRING OF OPINIONS ABOUT THE NATURE OF "INSPIRED PSALMODY"— GROSS ERRORS OF ROUSE.

MY DEAR SIR:—In pressing their demand that nine tenths of the churches in this country should abandon their cherished usages, and go over to the other *tenth*, viz. the friends of Rouse, one of the most popular arguments takes this form: "You have no *conscientious scruples* in regard to the one hundred and fifty Psalms of the Bible. In perfect consistency with your position you can admit our practice *to be in itself right*—but in consistency with our views, we advocates of Rouse cannot so regard your practice. You can sing the Psalms of David, but we cannot use your Psalmody." And the inference seems to be, that for the sake *of union*, the great body of the evangelical church should conform to the small fragment of the defenders of Rouse, by adopting their exclusive theory.

Now without pausing to remark upon the *modesty* of all this, but putting the case in its strongest shape, suppose that these brethren really sing "the inspired Psalms," not an explanatory paraphrase; concede for a moment that the real question is *not* (what we have shown it to be,) between "the paraphrase of Rouse" and the paraphrase of Dr. Watts, amended by our Assembly. Admitting all this for argument, this popular plea proceeds upon several obvious mistakes:

1. We do not admit either their *principle* or their practice "to be in itself right." The principle which assumes a Divine warrant for singing "a literal version of the whole book of Psalms," we regard as both false and injurious to the best interests of the church under her present dispensation. That there is no such "Divine appointment" either in the precepts or the practice of our Lord and his apostles, has been proved, we trust, in former Letters. And this result is strongly sustained by the reasonableness of the thing itself. Take for example, the first, though not the *most striking* illustration that presents itself: "Thou desirest not sacrifice, else would I give it—thou delightest not in burnt offering. The sacrifices of God are a broken spirit," &c.* Rouse gives the sentiment quite *literally*, and as far as it goes, nothing could be more appropriate. But is nothing more required of a Christian of these times? Here is the *version* sung by the Scottish Wishart the evening before his martyr-

* A parallel text is Psalm 66 : 15. "I will offer unto thee burnt sacrifices of fatlings, with the incense of rams; I will offer bullocks with goats." And so with very many others.

dom, and in the reformation times of John Knox, in parallel with our paraphrase:

WISHART'S HYMN.	DR. WATTS.
Gif thou had pleased sacrifice I should them offered thee; But thou wilt not sic sacrifice, For thou art wonder free: And givest us thy benefites Through Christ's blude freely. To thy mercie will I go.	A broken heart, my God, my king, Is all the sacrifice I bring— The God of grace will ne'er despise A broken heart for sacrifice. * * * * Thy blood can make me white as snow, No Jewish types could cleanse me so.

Indeed these brethren virtually admit this to be "the right practice," for in "explaining the Psalm," they teach the people to sing the *words* of Rouse with the very *meaning* adopted by Wishart and Watts! The *impiety* of attempting to improve the inspired song, is just as great in the one form as in the other—the difference being between improvement *in prose* and improvement *in verse*. And the distinct recognition of the only true sacrifice, "the Lamb of God," in this and other songs, we believe to be a duty—an essential method of "confessing Him before men." So the prophet Zechariah—"They shall look on ME whom they have pierced, and *mourn*."

2. We have much stronger objections to the *exclusive feature* of our brethren's "practice." While in themselves considered, there is no part of any of the one hundred and fifty Psalms which is absolutely *unfit* to be sung—there are unquestionably portions of many of those Psalms which are *less suitable* for New Testament worship than many other parts of the inspired Scriptures. And we have no hesitation in saying that it is *wrong, utterly* wrong to suffer such portions of the Psalms to *exclude* other more suitable and equally Divine ascriptions of praise from the private and public devotions of God's people. Take for instance those beautiful songs in the "Revelation." There can be scarce a doubt that the hymn, chapter 5 : 9–13, was intended to exhibit the na-

ture and characteristics of the New Testament Psalmody. Dr. Scott says — "Though *heaven* is the *scene of these visions*, yet they had continual reference to the temple and its worship; and *the state of the church* on earth is particularly adverted to." And what do they sing "*in heaven?*" Dr. Scott answers—"They all joined in a song of praise, which was not only most excellent, but it was also NEW, in respect of the *occasion* and *composition*: for the Old Testament church celebrated the praises of Jehovah, * * and anticipated *the coming* of the expected Messiah; but the New Testament church adored Christ *as actually come*, as having finished his work on earth * * * and entered into his glory." And so of other songs in that book. Yet these very songs of adoring wonder and love — "*Worthy is the* LAMB *that was slain*," &c.; these magnificent anthems sung with blessed voices and sinless hearts "in heaven," are pronounced "serious corruptions," if sung by the church on earth! We cannot but regard the principle which leads to such results as wrong, and *highly offensive* to "Him who sitteth on the throne, and to the Lamb." Yet the principle of these brethren, while it repudiates such songs as those mentioned, regards as highly acceptable such stanzas as the following:

Let covetous extortioners
Catch all he hath away:
Of all for which he labored hath,
Let strangers make a prey.

Let there be none to pity him,
Let there be none at all
That on his children fatherless
Will let his mercy fall.

Let God his father's wickedness
Still to remembrance call;
And never let his mother's sin
Be blotted out at all.

As cursing he like clothes put on,
Into his bowels so
Like water, and into his bones
Like oil, down let it go.

15

The New Testament interprets these passages as referring to the traitor Judas—and of course they belong to "the legal or prophetic language" of a previous economy, as Dr. Watts correctly explains them. But why should such stanzas be esteemed of "Divine appointment" and most acceptable praise, while the song of sublime triumph which John heard sung "in heaven" (Rev. 19 : 1–7,) over "the judgments" which "avenged the blood of God's servants" upon "the great whore" of the apostasy, would be a vile "corruption?"—"Alleluia, salvation and glory and honor and power unto the Lord our God." "And again they said, Alleluia. *Praise our God*, all ye his servants." "And I heard as it were the voice of a great multitude, and as the voice of many waters and of great thunderings, saying, Alleluia, for the Lord God omnipotent reigneth." "In these praises," says Dr. Scott, "the emblematical representatives of the church and her ministers *most cordially* united." Yes, they *could* unite "in heaven"—but these brethren *cannot unite* with the church on earth in such *a song!* "They are compelled to be silent," they tell us, "lest they should offer strange fire!"

3. That the "book of Psalms" was not designed by its Divine Author as the *Psalmody* of the church *exclusively* and for all coming time, appears most evident from a comparison of its contents with the substance, style and tenor of the New Testament, especially the Epistles. The new dispensation requires additional forms of worship, preaching, prayer and praise.

Probably no one will question that the writings of Paul and the other apostles form a *perfect standard* by which to construct our *prayers* and our *sermons*. How constantly and steadily is the attention fixed upon the CROSS! How does the glowing mind of the writer, especially of Paul, delight to place the crown upon the head of his Saviour? How does he love to dwell upon that *dear name* "which is above every name"—"that at the *name* of Jesus every knee should bow, and every tongue confess," &c. Thus, in the Epistle to the Ephesians, the titles Jesus, Christ, Jesus Christ, Lord Jesus Christ, Lord, Head, Master, Beloved, occur *sixty-three* times in one hundred and fifty-five verses; and in Philippians, *forty-three* times in one hundred and four verses. And *ascriptions of praise*, more or less direct, are offered to the adorable Redeemer, in not less than *twenty* instances in Ephesians—Philippians we have not examined. But the peculiar name JESUS, communicated to his mother by special revelation from God, is not found in the Psalms, and the term "*anointed*," Heb. *Messiah*, is not used to designate Christ more than six or seven times—though the volume contains between three thousand and four thousand verses—about *fifteen* times the number in the Epistles to the Ephesians and the Philippians.

The same train of remark applies to the third Person of the adorable Trinity. The three or four thousand verses of the Psalms mention the Holy Spirit not more than five or six times; but in the Ephesians alone, we find his name in connection with his Divine operations, *eleven* times. The New Testament economy is emphatically "the dispensation of the Spirit;" and therefore we may expect to discover much more full and precious demonstrations of his person, character, offices, attributes, and works; and this is especially true of his regenerating and sanctifying influences upon the hearts of men.

This contrast might be extended through all the great distinguishing doctrines and ordinances so clearly revealed in the new dispensation—all that is meant when it is said, "the law was given by Moses, but *grace and truth* came by Jesus Christ"—and "life and immortality are brought to light by the gospel." All devoted, able "ministers of the New Testament" feel alike on this topic; all recognize the teaching of Christ and his apostles as their chief pattern both in prayer and preaching, and even in "explaining the Psalms." Why should it be otherwise *in praise?* In these aspects we cannot but regard the practice of these brethren as very far from being *right;* and for such reasons as these, we cannot adopt their exclusive system of Psalmody, and especially not in a *literal* form. We feel conscientiously bound, in our measure to copy the inspired Paul, who often turns abruptly aside in the midst of his most logical trains of reasoning, to offer praise to his exalted Redeemer. For example, Rom. 9 : 5, "Of whom Christ came, who is over all, God blessed for ever. Amen."

4. We reach the same general result, when we examine many of the *prayers* embodied in "the Psalms." It has been shown, in our previous Letters, that no Divine command has indicated that book as *the only system* of song under the present dispensation. In regard to the very numerous prayers found in it, there is therefore no more reason why we should sing *literally* every expression of the Psalmist, than that we should use literally the other numerous prayers of the Bible, as of Solomon, Hezekiah, Jonah, Daniel, &c. Suppose a minister were to repeat literally, word for word, in the supplications of the pulpit, the prayer of Jonah, "Out of the belly of hell cried I." "I went down to the bottom of the mountains; the weeds were wrapped about my head." "Thou hadst cast me into the deep in the midst of the seas," &c. Such passages as these no doubt might be spiritualized (as Dr. Watts has done of parts of the Psalms) and used with a true "gospel sense," but we suppose no minister ever used this language in his prayers. And so of other prayers recorded in the Bible. They were composed for special occasions, and are universally regarded as unsuitable, and as never designed in their literal form for gospel worship.

A similar example presents itself, one of many, in the 59th Psalm. David speaks of his enemies thus:

At evening let thou them return,
Making great noise and sound,
Like to a dog, and often walk
About the city round.

Now whatever may have been the particular allusions

of the Psalmist, every one feels that the use *of this literal prayer in the pulpit* would be, to say the least, altogether inexpedient. With this judgment probably even the sticklers for the old version would coincide. Why then do they *sing it,* since the only difference is that in the latter case *they pray with a tune!* And so with scores of similar passages, which all will acknowledge to be *highly unsuitable for public formal prayer,* but which nevertheless they think highly appropriate for *public prayer with a tune!*

The great obscurity of many parts of the Psalms has led at least *one writer* to take the position "that it is not necessary *to understand what we sing* (or pray) in that book." * But if so, why not express the Hebrew in English letters and words, and sing *them?* By this method we would be sure of using "an inspired Psalmody." †

5. The great fundamental doctrine that JESUS OF NAZARETH WAS THE TRUE, THE LONG PROMISED MESSIAH, though nowhere taught in the Psalms, is often most emphatically inculcated in the New Testament. For assuming this character, he was bitterly persecuted by the Jews. "These things," says John, "are written that ye might believe that Jesus is the Christ." "Therefore," adds Peter, "let all the house of Israel know assuredly, that God hath made that same Jesus * * both Lord and Christ." And *the confession of* this great truth is exhibited by "the beloved disciple" as a test of true piety. "Many *deceivers* are entered into the world, who confess not that Jesus Christ is come in the flesh." "Hereby know ye the spirit of God — every spirit that confesseth that Jesus Christ is come in the flesh, is of God. And every spirit that confesseth not that Jesus Christ is come in the flesh, is *not of God.*" These are very strong declarations. And whatever else they teach, they at least

* Rev. Mr. Gordon.

† Thomas Aquinas held that it was not necessary for *first orders,* that a priest should understand the meaning of the Latin Mass Book; it was enough if he knew the words, and could pronounce them. Even the Council of Trent held the same.

condemn *any exclusive system* of praise which is defective in such essentials as these. We are far from insinuating that these brethren deny this fundamental of all religion — but so far as regards their *forms of praise,* they could not observe a more profound *silence* if no such doctrine were true. Even the malignant Jew finds no fault with their *confession* in this particular, but *unites* with them cordially! Can this be a full and scriptural compliance with the positive precept from heaven, viz. "that *all men should honor* THE SON even as they honor the Father?"

If it were necessary to multiply these objections, we might advert to the *fruits* of the system, of which *exclusive Psalmody* forms a prominent feature. We had the painful privilege, at the meeting of the Associate Synod in May, 1853, of being present at the trial of a complaint from the decision of a Presbytery, sent up by a minister of the gospel. The *high crimes* for which he had been arraigned, were these: 1. "Going to hear a minister of the Old School Presbyterians preach." 2. "Inviting to his pulpit an Associate Reformed clergyman!" For these offenses, the Presbytery was directed by the Synod to *proceed to trial!* What was the final result, we never took the trouble to ascertain.

Many of our readers are familiar with the action of the Synod of the Associate Reformed body, which confirmed the suspension of one of their elders for uniting in singing, at family worship, two verses of the 92d Psalm in our system, thus:

Sweet is the work, my God, my king,
To praise thy name, give thanks and sing, &c.

In his "Plea for Peace," Dr. M'Claren has shown that our version of this 92d Psalm is as good as Rouse's, though not perhaps quite so close. This case occurred in this vicinity. Yet at the very same meeting of Synod, several of the speakers declared that it was common, in both the Associate and Associate Reformed Synods, to receive members to communion, "who did not hold the doctrines of election and predestination." These facts demonstrate clearly which class of *offenses* belong "to the mint, cummin and anise," and which to "the weightier matters of the law."

A similar example was reported in "The Banner and Advocate," * by the person interested. He had been a Presbyterian; but having removed to Tipton county, Indiana, found it most convenient to unite with the Associate Reformed. Soon a particular friend in the Presbyterian ministry came along and preached in the neighborhood several times; also at the house of this gentleman. The Associate Reformed session got wind of it. He was accused of *being too sociable with Presbyterians,* hearing them preach, and uniting with them in singing. "This, they said, was a bad example that I was setting before the congregation, and as I was one of their leading members, others would be noticing these things; and that I would have to make some acknowledgments before I could have any church privilege. Not seeing that I had sinned against the All-wise Ruler of the universe, I was unwilling to confess that I had sinned against men: and the session accordingly *proceeded to discipline.*" One good result speedily followed—a new Presbyterian church was in a short time erected, dedicated and occupied by a promising congregation.

The explanation of such extreme measures as these is not difficult, on the principle stated by the late Dr. Claybaugh, of Oxford. In speaking of the state of denominational feeling existing in the Associate Reformed Synod of New York, he said: "It is believed that there is a growing conviction that, in order to maintain the life and energy of the body, *and prevent its being swallowed up* by the larger denominations, on the principle that in the moral as well as the material world the attraction of larger bodies is stronger than that of lesser bodies, the

* For January 22, 1859.

distinctive principles and rules of the body should be firmly maintained." *

Whether the maintaining of "distinctive rules" after the manner above indicated, will be promotive of the great interests of truth, charity, and salvation, is a very serious question. Ought not these brethren to fear lest religion herself should prove to be the sufferer from the scorn of a profane and wicked world?

There are venerable and excellent men in most denominations, whose very *prejudices* we instinctively regard with respect. From such a brother † proceeds the following: "Our views and usages *lean to virtue's side*—they originate in our fear of exalting *the human above the Divine.* Our error, if error it be, cannot be a dangerous one. It cannot arise from any disposition to slight the word of God." We regret to be obliged to take quite a different view of this subject. So long as Dr. M'D. sings "Rouse's paraphrase," interlarded, and if his views be correct, *corrupted* by hundreds of patches of "human composition," it is vain to talk about "the fear of exalting the *human* above the Divine." But waiving this—our esteemed brother *rejects,* "lays aside as useless," very many Psalms and hymns of the Bible, which even he will acknowledge to be inspired and Divine. For example, listen to Ralph Erskine, a chief captain of the Seceder host. He is speaking of the beautiful evangelical songs of Isaiah: "Of all the prophets (not excepting David,) none spoke *so clearly of Christ.* The whole of his prophecy * * * abounds with more poetical passages, sacred *odes* and evangelical *songs,* than *all* the other prophets besides (including David.) * * Those Divine hymns * * have in them as lofty and sublime strokes of poetry *as are to be met with.*" Now in these and scores of similar songs of praise in other parts of the Scriptures, there is nothing *human* for Dr. M'D.

* Preacher, July 12, 1854.

† Dr. M'Dill, of Sparta, Illinois.

to be *afraid of.* Erskine says he was not afraid of "turning these songs into metre *as the Psalms of David are, and for the same public use*"—because "it was so ordered by Act of the General Assembly of the church of Scotland in one of her most noted periods of her reformation;"* "and also by the Associate Synod, in 1747." In all this extensive department of inspired songs Dr. M'D's. fears of "exalting the human above the Divine" are utterly futile. Let him follow the safe leading of that venerable Seceder champion, and cast his *fears* to the winds. Or better still, let him be directed by the Act of the General Assembly of the church of Scotland, passed August 28, 1647, "that *noted period* of her reformation."

But there is another very dark side of this subject, where we fear *virtue* never leans. We have neither time nor space to speak at large of the lamentable, desolating evils which result so widely and injuriously, especially in the West, from "divisions about Psalmody." How often is a community split into fragments on this very rock of stumbling! Two or more poor shriveled churches, looking like Pharaoh's lean kine, drag out a miserable existence, the one denouncing the other as guilty of "idolatry," "offering strange fire before the Lord," "committing the sin of Nadab and Abihu," "laying the stepping stone for infidelity," "exposing themselves to the seven last plagues," "incurring the curse pronounced upon such as add to or take away from God's revealed word," &c. Thus they creep on from year to year, the one attempting to devour the other, neither able to sustain a pastor, or even to have preaching more than a half or quarter of the time. And what is the real source of the division? Why just this: Some preacher has taught the one party it is a *great sin* to use anything in Divine worship but the "book of Psalms." Of course, these people must "lean to virtue's side!" They must take good heed not "to exalt the human

* Erskine's Works, vol. 10, p. 425.

above the Divine," &c. Thus these two poor little churches wrap themselves up in their exclusiveness, the gospel is not preached, heresy spreads all around them, and souls perish by scores; whereas, if they were united, they could well support an efficient ministry, and become "a city set on a hill," a source and centre of Divine light and influence upon the whole neighborhood.

Is the foregoing picture too sombre in its coloring? We fear that in numerous instances it is not near so gloomy as the original. We believe these Psalmody divisions to be needless and sinful; and we as firmly hold that the exclusive system from which they spring is impracticable in theory, false in fact, and steadily tending to spread ruin among the souls of men.

Before closing this Letter, we wish to remark upon two or three topics, which have hitherto been deferred. Frequent allusion has been made to the scriptural doctrine of public and social prayer, especially as strictly of "human composition." Both prayer and praise agree in being a direct address to God, and the one is as near and solemn an approach to infinite purity as the other. Nor is there any greater *presumption* against the *right*, in itself considered, to compose our own praises, enlightened and assisted by the word and the Spirit of God (who is promised to "dwell with the church to the end of the world,") than to compose our own prayers. Suppose now a minister should make the following announcement to the people of his congregation—"Brethren, you may compose a prayer of any suitable length, the object of which shall be, in whole or in part, 'in your prayers to praise God.' You may select the materials in whole or in part from the New Testament; you may clothe it either in whole or in part in your own language; you may take it either in whole or in part from the book of Psalms or from other suitable parts of the Scriptures; and if you offer it in faith, or 'in the name of Christ,' you may assuredly expect the Divine blessing, and the acceptance of your offering. But, brethren, beware lest you be tempted to utter that same prayer with *a tune;* for if you dare to do so, you will commit a sin like unto the sin of 'Nadab and Abihu'—you will 'offer strange fire' and call down a curse upon your heads! You may '*speak* to God,' and 'in your prayers praise him' with such a 'human composition,' but if you dare to *sing* it, 'woe be unto you!'"

But it is said to be "most daring presumption and temerity" for any man to undertake to furnish "*matter to praise* the Great God in all that is imposing in his worship and service." * Yet we have precisely the same sources of "suitable matter," viz. the word, Spirit, providence and works of God, for *praise* as for *prayer.* And with the presence and aid of the Holy Spirit promised to the church, she has just as valid and perfect a right to compose a hymn, or approve it, when composed, and *sing* it, as to compose a prayer and *speak* it! She has *all the advantages* in the one case that she has in the other.†

Let us now compare the proprieties of praise with those which are acknowledged in the reading and preaching of the word. "In these latter exercises," says Matthew Henry, "God speaks to us—but in prayer (and praise) we speak to God." From these definitions we perceive why certain sentiments and passages of the Scriptures may be highly proper and suitable when God addresses us, or when we read or hear the Scriptures; and yet be much less suitable as the matter of our addresses to God, when we engage in praise and prayer. God, for example, may choose to address us by the pen

* Preacher, December 29, 1858.

† It has been said that "God has himself provided a *perfect system of praise*"—but that is the *very point* to be proved, not taken for granted! In regard to the New Testament and the new dispensation, *we deny the statement.* There are many very precious songs in the New Testament, but besides, there is a treasury of rich and varied materials for both praise and prayer; and to prepare and use these abundant provisions for the edification of her children, is the solemn duty of the church, whether in preaching the word, prayer or praise. This is what our General Assembly has done and is still doing.

of an inspired Jew, and by this instrumentality, living as he did under a dispensation of types and shadows, he may record for our instruction many matters pertaining to "burnt offerings," "incense of rams," "bullocks upon the altar," "organs," "timbrels," "dances," "cornets," "trumpets," "new moons," &c., and the holy resolutions of the pious of that day, to observe those typical rites and ceremonies, which were then commanded duties, may come down to us as the inspired record of the zeal, self-denial and holy fervor of the pious Jews. "The only wise God" thus chooses his own method of addressing us, expounded as it is by a further record—the Gospel dispensation taking the place of the Mosaic—the New Testament a commentary on the Old. But when we come to speak to God—to express "the *desires* of our hearts, in the name of Christ, and thankfully acknowledge his mercies," or perform the act of praise, "which terminates in God, and by which we confess and admire his perfections, works and benefits," circumstances are entirely changed. God may obviously speak to us in a manner and form in which it would be mockery and profaneness for us to speak to Him. It follows, therefore, that we may piously and profitably read or hear many many things found in the Scriptures which we may not employ, even though originally of a devotional nature, in speaking to God.

For example, how incongruous and improper would it be for a minister to introduce into a prayer the greater part of the 150th Psalm, as follows: "O God, we praise thee with the sound of a trumpet, we praise thee with stringed instruments and organs," &c. Indeed this is so obvious, and strikes the common sense of Christians so universally, that probably no person ever heard any minister of any denomination use such a prayer either in private or public. In the temple service these were commanded duties, and therefore their literal performance was a religious act, and a refusal to obey would have been sin. But now that that method of praising God with trumpets, high-sounding cymbals, organs, dances, is all done away, "to speak to God" in prayer, and "in our prayers to praise him," by expressing "our desire" or intention to employ this ancient service, "organs," "dances," &c., in his worship, all feel to be unsuitable; and probably no one ever ventured so far to disregard this common feeling of propriety in the sacred and solemn duty of prayer, unfolding as we do the most secret recesses of the heart to the Omniscient eye, as to make such an experiment upon the good sense and Christian conscientiousness of mankind. How then, we ask, can it be most suitable and proper for us to "speak to God" in praise, which is an equally solemn and direct address to the "Searcher of all hearts," language which we shrink from in the act of prayer? Nothing but common usage has sanctioned a distinction, where obviously there is no essential difference. We are far from supposing it necessary in all acceptable prayer and praise, "to assume every thought and expression for our own." But we maintain that if the *whole* book of Psalms is of Divine authority for *praise* literally, and in preference to all other inspired matter, its advocates fall into the foregoing difficulties and inconsistencies. No scriptural diversity between praise and prayer can explain or justify such incongruities.

In the foregoing Letters we have purposely avoided any extended comparison of the two versifications or "paraphrases" of the Psalms most commonly used. It has indeed been boldly asserted that we "exalt Watts above David." But it is scarcely necessary to point out the obvious distinction between the authorship of the Psalms, which all admit to be inspired, and the very humble part performed by the uninspired arranger of a poetical "paraphrase of the Psalms." God spake the Psalms by David—or David spake by the Holy Ghost. Dr. Watts writes a poetical *paraphrase* of the Psalms. Is he therefore a *better* writer than David? No more than Rouse is a *better writer* than David. No Presbyterian of ordinary sense ever conceived such a sentiment. It must have originated in another quarter.

On the other hand the theory and practice of our brethren appear to take almost as various hues as the chameleon. Thus in their "Testimony" they say—"We testify for the book of Psalms in a *faithful translation.*" * Dr. Cooper, on the contrary, says: "The only question is, has the translator observed the *order and arrangment* of the original, and is *the idea* fairly and fully brought out?" But this is to abandon entirely the principle of "a faithful translation." All Dr. C. contends for is "the inspired *order and arrangement*—and that the *idea* be fairly and fully brought out." On Dr. C's. principle, all his "explanations" of the Psalms before singing them, are *inspired*, provided he has observed the original "order and arrangement," and has fairly and fully *brought out* the idea"—conditions which he, of course, ordinarily observes. Besides, Dr. C's. principle condemns Rouse in *forty* or fifty gross departures from "the order and arrangement of the original." For illustrations, see a previous Letter. Dr. C. of course repudiates the *dictum* of his brother Dr. P., viz. that Rouse, "like the prose translation of the whole Bible, is substantially correct and faithful, and for the same reason, is to be regarded as the word of God!"—*Preacher,* Aug. 9, 1844.

Very different is the judgment of a writer in "The Christian Witness," a Seceder organ. He utterly rejects Dr. C's. theory, thus: "It may be said that such rhyming and syllabification *do not add to the ideas of the original.* So you may make a song or sermon out of a single sentence, without adding a single idea not contained in the text. But then you give us *not the pure word of God.*"

Indeed this latter writer candidly admits that the use of "redundant words, paraphrastic phrases, diminutive expressions," &c., such as Dr. C. approves, is a virtual surrender of the *whole question* of "inspired Psalmody." Thus he says: "If we may weaken the sense and add a

* Testimony United Presbyterian church, p. 46.

word to make a jingle; if we may impair the force, and cut off or supply a term or phrase, to make up the number of syllables in a line, or the number of lines in a verse, in order to please our fancy, may we not by the same process of reasoning, add a whole stanza, or make a *whole song of our own composition?*"

A similar view is taken in an article published in "The Preacher." * The writer says: "The permission to rhymers *to add and eke, and clip and twist the Holy Scriptures*, for the sake of a rhyming Psalmody, has opened a gate through which every sect, and every congregation, and every poet, afflicted with an itch of writing, has driven a hymn or a hymn book into the church of God. Now, truly, I see no good reason why one church *should have authority to give such permission, and another deprived of it.*" This of course condemns Rouse. If the Associate or Associate Reformed church, he says, "may add to the word of God *words of its own* sufficient to make half a dozen Psalms more or less," why may not others "add the matter of *a dozen!*" And the conclusion to which he comes emphatically is this: "All supporters of *rhyming Psalmody are disqualified for pleading the cause of an inspired Psalmody.*"

In closing his article, this writer plainly tells his brethren that they use a version *which has no authority* in the Bible. Hear him:

"We have no authority, then, from Scripture, for making or singing of rhyming Psalms; we are under no necessity to have or to use them."

But while some of these brethren, like the last writer, would repudiate Rouse (and every other system in rhyme) as *uninspired*, it still has zealous defenders. Thus Rev. Dr. Kerr: "We would have no more objection to a comparison of that which is known as Rouse's version, with the Psalms of David, than we would to a comparison of King James' translation of the Bible with the original Scripture."†

* For January 30, 1855.
† Preacher, August 9, 1847.

Thus we are back on the basis of the "Testimony," viz. "a faithful translation," "the unadulterated word of God," "songs composed in heaven!"

Nor do these brethren harmonize much better in regard to another aspect of the same subject. In a debate on the subject of "Improvement of Psalmody," in the Associate Synod, * Dr. Cooper said: "Something must be done. The interests of the church and the extension of our cause are involved. I refer members to a letter from brother Herron. He says we do not appreciate the matter here. We are familiar with this version, but it is not so elsewhere. He has great difficulty in persuading the people to make use of this version, owing to the awkwardness of the expressions. *They are becoming tired of it.* It makes me feel very unhappy when I think of the awkwardness of them, and know that they might be so easily improved. Those who have had any experience on this subject must feel the force of his objections. *Any poetry two hundred years old must be of such a character as to excite a smile.* The pronunciation and phraseology are altogether different from what they are now." So also a writer in the "United Presbyterian" "despairs of ever bringing the Catholic church back to David's Psalms," without a new and better version—and without such version, he adds, "we must rest content, either to give up a Divine appointment, or remain a little separated branch of the church to all coming generations."

That there are very serious doctrinal and historical errors in "Rouse's paraphrase," does not admit of a doubt. Thus Psalm 69 : 4 : "They that would destroy me, being mine enemies wrongfully, are mighty : then I restored that which I took not away." This Psalm is a most remarkable prophecy of the Messiah. "The Holy Spirit," observes Scott, "evidently spoke of the sufferings of Christ, and the glory that should follow. Indeed it is so manifest a prophecy of Christ, that we should consider

* May, 1854.

him as the speaker in most parts of it." How then has Rouse paraphrased the verse quoted above?

They that would me destroy, and are
Mine enemies wrongfully,
Are mighty: so that I took not
To render *forced was I.*

"Christ made satisfaction for our sins, and restored that honor to the Divine law which he had not taken away."—*Scott.* But was Christ "*forced*" to do this? Was he *forced* to make satisfaction for sinners? To suppose this is to overthrow the essential nature of the Divine sacrifice; to misrepresent the inspired record, and to contradict the Saviour himself: "I lay down my life for the sheep. No man taketh it from me, but I lay it down of myself."

The rendering in our system is liable to none of these objections:

'Twas then I paid that dreadful debt
Which men could never pay,
And gave those honors to thy law,
Which sinners took away.

The following from Psalm 18:25, is nearly as unintelligible to most persons as the Hebrew:

Thou gracious to the gracious art,
To upright men upright:
Pure to the pure, froward thou kyth'st
Unto the froward wight.

We cannot enter into further details. But in closing this Letter we respectfully ask, ought not the arguments and facts of this and previous discussions to lead these brethren seriously to reflect upon certain moral aspects of their position? Have they not virtually CUT OFF from the church of Christ, the Free church, the Established church, and all the other Scottish Presbyterian churches, except a small "fraction." I say *virtually*—for of course they have not the *power.* But is not this the fair and legitimate result of their exclusive principles and practice? Yes, if Dr. Candlish or Dr. Cunningham were to come to this country, they could not be admitted to commune with these brethren! Certainly not, if they would treat those distinguished persons as they do their own elders, who sing "the mere productions of men."

LETTER XIV.

MISREPRESENTATIONS OF DR. WATTS EXPOSED — THE USE OF HYMNS IN THE PRIMITIVE CHURCH, PROVED BY DR. M'MASTER, MERLE D'AUBIGNE, NORTH BRITISH REVIEW, NEANDER, AND OTHERS — LETTER OF PLINY — TESTIMONY OF EUSEBIUS — HYMNS CONDEMNED BY THE COUNCIL OF LAODICEA, WHICH ALSO FORBID ANY TO SING EXCEPT THE CHORISTERS — CASE OF THE HERETIC PAUL OF SAMOSATA — TRUTHS ESTABLISHED BY THAT CASE.

MY DEAR SIR:—In this, my closing Letter, I propose to examine with some care various injurious charges made against the memory of Dr. Watts, and intended to reflect odium upon those who employ his poetical labors in the worship of God. In view of the principles and arguments of former Letters, how strange that men of piety and sense, who have written much on these topics, should utter such a sentiment as this: "The principle which maintains that *these Psalms* (of David) are not suitable to be employed in the worship of the church under the gospel dispensation, is a discovery of modern times." * But who maintains such a principle? Certainly no Presbyterian. Dr. Watts and some others have said this in regard *to certain parts* of the Psalms — but never, to the best of my knowledge, of "*the Psalms*" as a whole. See how easy by a *little twist* of this sort, to caricature the sentiments of any man or set of men?

A similar mis-statement represents Dr. W. as having

* Pressly on Psalmody, p. 6.

"*conceived the idea* that the Psalms as given by inspiration, (observe, *the Psalms*, the *whole Psalms!*) are unfit to be sung."* Here is a similar perversion. Again, Dr. K. tells us—"Isaac Watts conceived the idea * * that GENERALLY they (i. e., the Psalms as given by inspiration) tended to 'sink our devotion and hurt our praise.'" In reply, I again deny the statement as a matter of fact. Isaac Watts never "conceived such an idea." The words as partly quoted, are at the close of an argument in which Dr. Watts expressly says he is speaking of "several passages," and "the application of many verses of David;" he is speaking of "the omission of whole lines and verses," by a certain class of intelligent singers; "whereas," he adds, "the more unthinking go singing in cheerful ignorance wherever the clerk (or precentor) leads them, across the river Jordan, through the land Gebal, Ammon, and Amelek; * * they enter into the temple, they bind their sacrifices with cords to the horns of the altar, they join with the high-sounding cymbals, their thoughts are bedarkened with the smoke of incense and covered with Jewish veils." Now it is of these *special* circumstances and expressions that Dr. Watts says—"I fear they do but sink our devotion and hurt our worship." Is this the same as saying that "GENERALLY they (the Psalms) tend to sink our devotion and hurt our praise!" Dr. Watts is speaking of certain special Jewish peculiarities which he admits to be "the beauties and perfections of a Hebrew song, and adapted by Infinite Wisdom to raise the affections of the saints of that day"—but in his judgment adapted "to sink the devotion" of Christians at the present time. Dr. Watts' design and reference were to these special and peculiar features of a *part* of the Psalms—the editor of the "Preacher" quotes his words as applicable to the Psalms *generally!* Is this a fair and righteous use of the words?

We have already stated that the Presbyterian church has never sanctioned Dr. Watts' prose writings, nor is

* Preacher, September 15, 1852.

she responsible for their sentiments. They may be right or wrong, true or false—they are not ours. When, therefore, with great parade and triumph certain objectionable statements are quoted against us from those writings, this can scarcely be reconciled with the principles of fair and honorable discussion, which should govern all, especially Christians. This is true, even when the views of Dr. W. are correctly quoted—much more when they are perverted as above.

Again—Dr. Watts is charged with "using arguments not only unsatisfactory, but impious," because he says he kept his "grand design in view, viz. 'to teach his author to speak like a Christian,' or 'the common sense (or experience) of a Christian.'" But let Dr. W. explain his own meaning. "My design is," he says, "to accommodate the book of Psalms to Christian (in opposition to Jewish) worship. And in order to this, it is necessary to divest David, Asaph, &c., of every *other character* but that of a Psalmist and a *saint*, and to make them always speak the common sense (or experience) of a Christian." In other words, he designed that David should "leave Judaism behind," instead of praising God with "incense of *rams, trumpets, cornets, dances*," &c. So also in another oft-quoted and much abused passage, where he says that "David should be converted into a Christian;" yet in *the very same sentence* he explains himself, as follows, viz. "that a good part of the Psalms should be fitted for the use of the churches" in "*a paraphrase in which dark expressions should be enlightened, Levitical ceremonies and Hebrew forms of speech changed into the worship of the gospel, and explained* (as certain preachers do) in the language of our time and nation." This is what Dr. Watts meant by teaching "David to speak the common sense of a Christian," and "converting him into a Christian."

We do not defend the use of this phraseology—"converting David into a Christian." It sounds harshly, though in the same style with the expression, "teach the

Psalmist to speak English," i. e., by "translation." * Yet a very little candor would satisfy any intelligent man that his *meaning* was unexceptionable : "For why should I now address God my Saviour in a song, with burnt sacrifices of fatlings and with the incense of rams? Why should I pray to be sprinkled with hyssop, or recur to the blood of bullocks and goats? Why should I bind my sacrifices with cords to the horns of the altar?" &c. By teaching his "author to speak like a Christian," Dr. Watts therefore plainly refers to Christianity as opposed to Judaism; and means precisely what Dr. Pressly practices every Sabbath morning when he explains a Psalm containing these ceremonial and Jewish expressions! And yet Dr. P. has the boldness to ask—"Does not Dr. Watts virtually arraign the wisdom of the Holy One of Israel and undertake to teach him 'to speak like a Christian?'" We reply—Does not Dr. P. "virtually arraign the wisdom of the Holy One of Israel" when in explaining these passages of the Psalms, he teaches the people to sing them as he interprets them by the New Testament? Is not this conduct of Dr. P. quite as "derogatory to the Spirit of Inspiration" as the language of Dr. Watts?

"It would appear then," adds Dr. P., "that in the estimation of this man (Dr. W.) the teaching of the Holy Spirit which the Psalmist enjoyed was very insufficient, and that it was necessary that one in modern times should undertake the office of teaching him 'to speak like a Christian.'" † Well, as Dr. P. constantly practices this *teaching* of the Psalmist, we hope he will not henceforth be very severe on Dr. Watts — especially as the chief difference between the two sorts of teaching is, that Dr. P. teaches in *prose*, but Dr. W. in *poetry!*

Again, Dr. W. is charged with affirming that parts of the Psalms "tend to excite unholy passions," and "ex-

* Here is a parallel case: "Luther * * * undertook the difficult task of making these Divine teachers (the apostles, &c.) speak his mother tongue." *D'Aubigne, History of the Reformation*, vol. 3, p. 31.

† Pressly on Psalmody, p. 110.

press resentment and hatred against the Psalmist's personal enemies." * Thus he says, "Among the imprecations that David uses against his adversaries in the Psalm (35th) I have endeavored to turn the edge of some of them from personal enemies against the implacable enemies of God in the world." On this last passage Dr. P. remarks—"Here the reader will see that David is supposed to have uttered imprecations against personal enemies. Could he, then, have been under the influence of the Holy Spirit?" We reply—certainly the Psalmist could not "have been under the influence of the Holy Spirit," if his imprecations were directed against those who were his personal enemies, considered in his *private character as a member of society; or if he was governed by feelings of private revenge. But was not David a king? Did he not shed much blood? Did he not sustain the character of a judge in Israel, as also that of an eminent protector of the church?* Were not the heathen around "his adversaries" in all these respects? Or does Dr. P. think it equally *unchristian to "utter imprecations against enemies"* in any of these relations? Take for example, the familiar case of David and Goliah. Does Dr. Pressly think it was "unchristian" in David to pray that Goliah might be slain? Was not Goliah his adversary, acting as David did in the person of a defender of his nation and his church? Or to go farther back, did not Joshua and the judges "utter imprecations" against their "adversaries" whom they were commanded to exterminate, certainly not as private individuals, but as public persons?

So also when David uses the following prayer, we perceive what Dr. Watts means by "sharp invectives against personal enemies," and "imprecations against David's adversaries." "*Consume them in wrath, consume them that they may not be.*" Psalm 59 : 13. "In this Psalm," remarks Dr. Scott, "David expresses what his thoughts and affections were, when Saul sent officers to watch his

* Pressly on Psalmody, p. 99.

house all night, to slay him." And on the 13th verse quoted above he adds — "It is probable that David meant the disgrace, degradation, and gradual extirpation of Saul's family, for their opposition to the Lord's anointed (David himself) and all their imprecations and calumnies against him." This is precisely what Dr. Watts means by "David's personal enemies"—viz. enemies to his person as the King of the Jews, or ordained to be so—enemies to his throne, and to his life, &c.

These examples also show the meaning of Dr. W. when he speaks of "some dreadful *curse against men* proposed to our lips, which is so contrary to the new commandment of loving our enemies," and "almost opposite to the spirit of the gospel." Certainly Dr. W. is right in affirming that there is nothing in "the spirit of the gospel" requiring us to destroy and exterminate the heathen, as was the duty of Joshua and David. "Why," remarks Dr. W., "why must I join with David in *his legal or prophetic language,* to curse my enemies, when my Saviour in his sermons has taught me to love and bless them?" The reader will observe the qualifying clause—"*in his legal or prophetic language.*" Take a few examples from the Psalms. "*He teacheth my hands to war,* so that a bow of steel is broken by my hands. *I have wounded them that they were not able to rise:* they are fallen under my feet. Thou hast given me the necks of my enemies; that I might *destroy them that hate me.* Arise, O Lord, disappoint him, cast him down. When my enemies are turned back they shall fall and perish at thy presence."

There are scores, perhaps hundreds of similar passages, some of them much stronger in expression. To David, as the anointed king and captain of God's people, they were highly appropriate. To that "legal" or ceremonial dispensation, when it *was David's duty to fight and exterminate* the surrounding heathen nations, this language was most suitable. "But," argues Dr. Watts, "as no such duties now devolve upon Christians, why must they 'join with David in this legal or prophetic language?' I cannot use it against 'my enemies,' for I am commanded 'to pray for and bless them.' Why, then, should I use David's language toward foes *long since dead*, and which at best, was 'legal or prophetic,' and thus altogether peculiar to that people, day and dispensation?"

These illustrations also explain Dr. Watts' meaning when he represents "persons of seriousness as forced to omit whole lines and verses, because they dare not sing *without understanding*, and almost against their consciences." "I have left out," he adds, "some whole Psalms, and several parts of others, that tend to fill the mind with overwhelming sorrows or sharp resentments." The meaning of this is already explained. The reason which governed Dr. Watts in these omissions, Dr. P. says is this—"Some of them (the Psalms) are of dangerous tendency!" But where has Dr. Watts said so?

"We meet a line," he says, "which belongs but to one action or hour of the life of David, that breaks off our song in the midst; our consciences are affrighted lest we should *speak a falsehood* unto God * * * before we have time to reflect that this may *be sung only as a history of ancient saints*." "There are a thousand lines in it (the book of Psalms) which were not made for a church in our days *to assume as its own*." Dr. W. speaks of the dark, "carnal," shadowy dispensation of Judaism, which Dr. Owen says "gave no clear and distinct apprehensions of the future state of glory." But is this the same as to say that the Psalms which treat of that dispensation "are of dangerous tendency." He agrees with Dr. Jno. Owen, that the Jewish system of "worship was carnal and outwardly pompous"—also that certain parts of "these Psalms of Jewish composure ought to be translated for Christian worship," and that some of them, and parts of others, may be properly omitted, as never having been designed by their Divine Author for the purposes of praise under the gospel.

But is this the same as "slandering the Holy Spirit or offering a fearful indignity to the Spirit of Inspiration." * These examples will serve to show with how much truth Dr. W. is charged with representing "the Psalmist as giving vent to *feelings of malevolence toward his personal enemies*," &c. He admits that to persons who "*have not time to reflect*" how certain parts may be properly sung (viz. "as a history of ancient saints,") the tendency may be to produce "overwhelming sorrows and sharp resentments." But he adduces this rather as an abuse, which ought to be corrected, than a legitimate result from the right use of the Psalms.

But it is in his versification of the 119th Psalm that Dr. Watts is affirmed to have treated the writings of the Holy Spirit with special indignity! "I have collected and disposed," he says, "the most useful verses of this Psalm under eighteen different heads, and formed a Divine song on each of them; but the verses are much transposed to attain some degree of connection." Dr. P. considers this as indicating that he could not have regarded the Psalm as "the production of Infinite Wisdom." "Is the mind of the Spirit," he asks, "*exhibited so awkwardly* as to render it necessary that the verses should be much transposed to attain *some* degree of connection?" † But here Dr. P. exhibits much more zeal than wisdom or prudence. We know nothing is more common in the pulpit than to classify and group under heads the members of a paragraph. Thus in the Epistles, the rapid intellect of the apostle Paul, under the Divine inspiration, passes with admirable vehemence over the parts of a great subject, so that in lecturing on his writings, it often greatly aids in understanding the sense, to have such a grouping together of topics. Yet the preacher or lecturer does not suppose he is thereby insulting the Holy Spirit! So in the book of Proverbs, many whole chapters are made up of separate sentences, whose connection it is very difficult to

* Prossly on Psalmody, pp. 99, 100, 71.
† Ibid, p. 114.

perceive. Thus, also, in the 119th Psalm, the eminently pious and practical Matthew Henry says, "There is *seldom any coherence between the verses*, but like Solomon's Proverbs, it is a chest of gold rings, 'not a chain of gold links.'" But if Dr. P. is correct, Matthew Henry must have believed the book of Proverbs, as well as this Psalm, "to be very *awkwardly exhibited* by the Holy Spirit!" To such extravagance will men rush in pursuit of some favorite notion.

It is obvious, therefore, that in grouping the verses of this Psalm under eighteen heads, according to *topics*, Dr. W. has done nothing worse than Dr. P. himself does, when he lectures on other parts of the Scriptures; nothing which Henry does not admit to be necessary and proper on account of the want of "coherence between the verses." Nor is Watts more to blame than Henry and Pressly! Certainly what is plain sober sense in Matthew Henry, cannot be so horribly impious in Dr. Watts! Among one hundred and seventy-six verses, which Henry says "seldom have any coherence," nearly all spoken of the law of God, Watts has classified those which from their meaning seem properly to fall together. His object was good — not to offer insult to the Holy Spirit, but to aid the feeble understandings of men in their attempts to show forth the praises of the infinite and incomprehensible God. Where two or more verses were exactly or nearly in the same terms, he classified them together, &c. In all this he did precisely what every able lecturer on the Holy Scriptures does in the pulpit, in another part of public worship, to explain, apply and honor the blessed truth of God.

"But," inquires Dr. P., "shall a sinful mortal select such verses as he considers 'most useful,' and pass over the remainder as unworthy of notice?" * But does not Dr. P. "*pass over*" the 20th verse of Psalm 72, and reject it from his Psalmody? Does not he, "a sinful mortal, *pass over*" a number of other parts of the Psalms, espe-

* Pressly on Psalmody, p. 114.

cially most of the inspired titles? Does he not "pass over" all the other "inspired Psalms, hymns and spiritual songs" in Isaiah and the other prophets, &c., as "unworthy of notice" in his system of praise! As to the *sin* of transposition, we have already shown that there are *thirty* or *forty* such cases in Rouse! Did he "*know better* than the Holy Spirit *the order*," &c.?

Again, Dr. Watts is quoted as saying, that "he is bold to maintain the great principle" of his work, "that if the brightest genius on earth, or an angel from heaven, should *translate* David, and keep close to the *sense*, he could not make a suitable Psalm book." *

From this Dr. K. infers that Watts did not design to give the "correct sense of David." But is there no *restriction* in Dr. Watts' language? What is the fact? The paragraph quoted, opens thus: "I must confess I have never seen any version or paraphrase *of the Psalms in their own* JEWISH SENSE, so perfect as to discourage all further attempts. But whoever undertakes the *noble work*, let him bring with him *a soul devoted to piety*, an exalted genius, and withal a studious application. For David's harp abhors a profane finger," &c. Then a few lines farther down in the same paragraph, comes the extract mutilated by the "Preacher:" "But still I am bold to maintain the great principle on which my present work is founded; and that is, that if the brightest genius on earth, or an angel from heaven, should translate David, and keep *close to the sense and style of the inspired author*, we should only obtain thereby a bright and heavenly copy *of the devotions of the Jewish king*, but it could never make the fittest Psalm book for a Christian people;" i. e., for the gospel church.

No comments are necessary to point out the distinctly limited meaning of Dr. Watts. He is speaking of "the Jewish sense" of the Psalms—he regards them as they are, "the devotions of the Jewish king"—and it is in this view he says he does not design "to keep close to

* Dr. Kerr, in Preacher.

the sense and style of the inspired author!" Yet who would ever dream that this was his meaning from the extract made by the "Preacher?" But when this is made known it spoils the whole argument. Whether this is fair treatment of an author, others can decide.

Again, I quote from a printed volume thus: "Dr. Watts, whose compositions are sung in public and family worship by a great majority of professed Christians in the United States, maintained that *the Psalms* were too Jewish to be sung with edification by Christians." "And the idea is very prevalent that *the book of Psalms* is not adapted to Christian worship."

Both these extracts are *untrue*. Dr. Watts maintained that "*a part* of the Psalms are too Jewish," and "the idea is prevalent," not *that* "*the book* of Psalms," but parts of the Psalms "are not adapted to worship" under the gospel.

But we cannot extend these illustrations. They show what most unrighteous judgment Dr. Watts has received. His paraphrase of the Psalms is "the mere production of an English poet"—he is charged with having "advanced principles which strike at the *inspiration* of the Scriptures," * and with "speaking reproachfully of the Psalms." With what small show of reason these assaults are made, the foregoing examples will prove. In his "Treatise on Prayer," he uses this language: "If we find our hearts very barren, and hardly know how to frame a prayer before God of ourselves, it has been oftentimes useful to take a book in our hand, wherein are contained some spiritual meditations in a petitionary form, some devout reflections, or excellent patterns of prayer; and *above all*, THE PSALMS OF DAVID, some of the prophecies of Isaiah, some chapters in the gospels or any of the epistles. Thus we may lift up our hearts to God," &c. "Above all, the Psalms of David!"—And yet we are told that Dr. Watts "spoke disparagingly of the book of Psalms!" And in his "Advice to a Young Man," he

* Pressly on Psalmody, p. 51.

says: "To direct your carriage toward God, converse particularly with the book of Psalms." Instead of being "the mere effusions of men," nothing would be easier than to prove by actual comparison, that in a large number of his versifications, he has given all *that is inspired* in the Psalm, viz. not the very language of our prose translation, which was the work of uninspired men; not the poetry of Rouse, but *the sentiments* doctrinal and devotional, as fully and fairly brought out in our system as in that of Rouse.

As to the rest, Dr. W. says: "I think I may assume the pleasure of being the first who hath brought down the royal author into the common affairs of the Christian life, and led the Psalmist of Israel *into the church* of Christ *without anything of a Jew about him.*" Yet there are those who assert that it was Dr. W's. intention "impiously to reject the Psalmist from the church !"

We admit, with the "North British Review," "that in his old age" Dr. Watts *unfortunately* attempted "to set philosophers right on the subjects of space, liberty and necessity, and even sought to re-adjust, for theologians, the doctrine of the Trinity." * It was "in his old age"—when in some degree borne down by years and bodily infirmity. But in his "Preface to his Lyric Poems," he speaks of "the eternal God becoming an infant of days, * * * agonies of sorrow loading the soul of him who was God over all, and the Sovereign of life stretching his arms on a cross, bleeding and expiring." What could be more full and explicit than these stanzas from the 45th and 63d of his hymns:

See where the great incarnate God
  Fills a majestic throne,
While from the skies his awful voice
  Bears the last judgment down—

I am the first, and I the last,
  Through endless years the same;
I am, is my memorial still,
  And my eternal name.

* North British Review, for August, 1857.

What equal honors shall we bring
To Thee, O Lord our God the Lamb,
When all the notes that angels sing
Are far inferior to thy name.

These are but specimens of many pages of the same import, which might be extracted from his writings. Nor is he less explicit in regard to the distinct personality and divinity of the Holy Spirit.

In Dr. Watts' work on the Trinity, published after his Psalms and Hymns, he says:

"1. Those very *names, titles, attributes, works* and *worship*, which are peculiar to God, and incommunicable to another, are ascribed to THREE, by God himself, in his word; which three are distinguished by the names of FATHER, SON and SPIRIT.

"2. There are, also, some other circumstantial, but convincing evidences, that the SON and the SPIRIT have the true and proper Godhead ascribed to them, as well as the FATHER.

"3. Thence it necessarily follows, that these *three*, viz. the FATHER, SON and HOLY SPIRIT, have such an intimate and real communion in that ONE GODHEAD, as is sufficient to justify the ascription of those peculiar and distinguishing Divine characters to them.

"4. Though the FATHER, SON and SPIRIT are but *one* God, yet there are such distinct properties, actions, characters and circumstances ascribed to these THREE, as are usually ascribed to *three distinct* PERSONS *among men.*"

In our Letter No. XII., reference was made to the ancient literature of hymns. A few further suggestions and some quotations from recent publications, are all that our space permits.

1. Dr. M'Master, author of the "Apology for the book of Psalms," admits "the existence of hymns of human composition at *an early day*, and their use in the church," he adds, "is with *us no matter of dispute*"— "they were frequently used in public worship," &c. *

* Apology, p. 34.

2. Another important witness to the same truth, is the eminent Merle D'Aubigne, the learned author of "The History of the Reformation of the Sixteenth Century." In that wonderful revolution which shook the Papacy to its foundations, "men could not confine themselves," he says, "to mere translations of ancient hymns. The souls of Luther and many of his cotemporaries * * * poured forth their feelings in religious songs. * * * Thus the hymns were revived, which in THE FIRST CENTURY had *consoled the pangs* of the martyrs." In these, he tells us, "poetry and music blended their most heavenly features." * The distinguished historian traces these "hymns of human composure" back to the very period of primitive Christianity, "the first century."

3. A third important witness is the "North British Review." After quoting from the earliest historian of the church, † who has preserved "a fragment of the second century," the hymn beginning, "We praise thee, we bless thee," &c., the Review adds, "this hymn is invested with a charm, * * * for it was the song which martyr after martyr sang so cheerfully as they marched from prison to their death place." ‡

The same authority, after citing a number of ancient hymns by Ephream the Syrian, uses the following language:

"In many cases, hymns like these were *the sole conservatives of gospel truth* when heterodoxy grew and flourished beneath the Papal influence. They *were too pure* to be defiled by Romish contaminations, * * * they have come down to us in all the splendor of their first purity. * * * We ought to love them the more, because they flowed with *clear and living streams* through the barren wastes of Popery." ||

This threefold testimony (Dr. M'Master, Merle D'Au-

* History of Reformation, vol. 3, p. 177.
† Eusebius, Ecclesiastical History, b. 28.
‡ North British Review, August, 1857.
|| Ibid.

bigne and the North British Review) furnishes a full and triumphant reply to the vaunting challenge so rashly put forth and repeated, as follows: "If you can find a single instance from the day *that heard the melodies of the sweet singer of God's Israel*, on down to the day that heard the horrible blasphemies of Paul of Samosata, *of a single church member*, who *on one solitary occasion* used in God's worship *any other* than the hymns contained in the book usually called the 'Psalms of David,' then I will give up this whole controversy." *

If any further authority is required, we have it in the illustrious Neander, the prince of modern church historians—"The Psalmody of the early church consisted in part of the Psalms of David, and *in part of hymns* composed for the purpose." † Nor does ecclesiastical history for the first four centuries present so much as *a fragment* of evidence that any individual or Council made objection to these hymns until we come to the Synod of Laodicea, A. D. 344–346. That Synod passed an act prohibiting "*all hymns* as of dangerous tendency, and restricting their churches to the Psalter and *other canonical songs* of the Scriptures." ‡ The Synod, it seems, tolerated "*the other songs* of Scripture," which our brethren call "corruptions." But the historian adds this significant clause—"The ARIANS of that age also *opposed* these ancient hymns, *for different reasons*." ‖ The reason is not given, but perhaps the present practice of the Arians of Ulster in retaining Rouse may suggest an explanation.

The celebrated letter of Pliny to the Emperor Trajan (A. D. 103–4) states that having tortured several of the Christians, he discovered no other crime in their assemblies, than that "they were accustomed to meet before

* United Presbyterian, of Cincinnati.

† Allgem. Kirsch.

‡ Neander says that the same Synod, in the 15th canon, "ordered that *no one should sing* at Divine service, except the choristers."—*Biblical Repertory*, January, 1832.

‖ Primitive Church, by Coleman, p. 376.

day, *carmen Christo quasi Deo secum dicere invicem*—"to sing to Christ as God in alternate responses." Tertullian, a century later, referring to this letter of Pliny, says—"Every one was invited in their public worship to sing unto God, *according to his ability, de proprio ingenio*—a song composed by himself, or one selected from the Scriptures." * Those who possessed poetical talent, prepared suitable hymns, and recited them in the public assemblies.

The historian Eusebius, also quotes Caius, a cotemporary of Tertullian, thus—"Who knows not * * * how many songs and odes of the brethren there are, written *from the beginning, jam pridem*—'a long time ago,' by believers, and offering praise to Christ as the word of God, ascribing divinity to him." † Many of these hymns were preserved and appealed to in subsequent ages in the controversies with the Arians and other enemies of the truth. ‡ Origen, who flourished A. D. 250, Dyonisius, and other early writers, often cited these hymns as a sort of common literature of the church, and thus confounded the errorists.

The case of the arch-heretic Paul of Samosata, who was deposed for denying the divinity of Christ, and other offenses, by the Council of Antioch, A. D. 269, has been often employed in this controversy. The decision of the Council, translated from Eusebius by Milner, so far as it refers to Psalmody, is as follows: "He suppressed the Psalms made in honor of Jesus Christ, and called them modern compositions—and he directed others to be sung in the church in his own commendation." || Neander states the facts thus—"The church hymns which had been in use since the second century, he banished as an innovation, * * * on the principle *that only passages out of the Holy Scripture ought to be sung;* and thus he

* See his Apology, c. 8.
† Ecclesiastical History, lib. 5: 28.
‡ See Neander.
|| Ecclesiastical History, vol. 1, p. 230.

probably suffered nothing but the Psalms to be used." This opposition to "the church hymns" by the heretic Paul, as well as his agreement with the Arians of the period of the Council of Laodicea, in preferring the naked Psalms, is not difficult of explanation. Why do all such heretics of the present day hate and oppose creeds and confessions? Why do they denounce them as profane additions to the word of God, which they claim as *the only and all-sufficient* creed? They all profess, like Arius, when arraigned before the Council of Nice (A. D. 325), to believe the Scriptures. "But it soon appeared," says Milner, "that without *some explanatory terms* decisively pointing out what the Scriptures had revealed, it was impossible to guard against the subtleties of the Arians." * They were ready to adopt the strongest terms employed in the Scriptures to designate the divinity of Christ, even "God"—"the true God," &c., because they received them with their own interpretations. But the Council at length drove Arius and his party out of all their hiding places, by employing such forms of confessing Christ as even the arch-heretic could not receive.

In these facts we discover the secret of the hostility of Paul and his friends to the "hymns of the churches," and their decided preference for the naked text of David—just as the Jew and the modern Arian are quite willing to sing the simple words of the second Psalm—but what Jew would accept for worship Dr. Watts' paraphrase of it? And the same is true of the Arian. But is not this the same as saying that the inspired Psalms are adapted to the propagation of fundamental error? No more than the same thing is asserted of *the whole Scriptures* by all who employ creeds as tests of soundness in the faith. Painful facts prove that the Holy Scriptures are not a sufficient safeguard against the intrusion of heresy—and therefore other tests are adopted. What is true of the sacred VOLUME, is true of all its

* Ecclesiastical History, vol. 1, p. 280

parts, even of the Psalms. Paul and his Arian brethren knew this, and, therefore, they had the same preference for those Psalms over the more explicit "hymns of the church," as modern heretics express for "THE BIBLE AS THEIR CREED," over the acknowledged symbols of sound Protestant churches. For such reasons as these, the heretic Paul of Samosata "banished the church hymns," which expressly and beyond all controversy ascribed divinity to Christ, and he adopted the "principle *that only passages of Scripture ought to be sung*, and probably suffered nothing but Psalms (of David) to be used." Such is the testimony of Neander, the greatest of modern historians. As to Paul's having on one occasion (Easter) required hymns to be sung in *his own praise*, it was a separate offense, and so dealt with by the Council. It is not intimated that such was his common practice, nor that he *ordinarily* enjoined songs in honor of himself, in the room of the worship of God. In view of such evidence as this, we leave the reader to decide between Dr. Pressly and Dr. M'Master; the former of whom says, that "the daring impiety of Paul was manifested in his taking such liberty with the Psalms whose author is the Holy Spirit"—but the latter (Dr. M'M.) says—"Paulus refused to celebrate the Deity of Christ in a *modern hymn*." * The whole history of ancient hymnology goes to establish the truth of the statement of Neander, and he but expresses the views of the translator of Mosheim, and of all ecclesiastical historians, so far as familiar to the writer. The recent attempt to give the subject a different aspect, arose out of the exigencies of the Psalmody controversy.

The case of Paul of Samosata possesses importance in this discussion, from the following truths, which it clearly establishes:

1. Paul found in common use, certain "church hymns,"

* Paulus probably found "less difficulty in accommodating or perverting the Biblical Psalms to his Socinian opinions, than the modern hymns composed expressly in honor of the Son of God."—*Biblical Repertory*, 1829.

handed down from the second century, perhaps of even earlier date.

2. These hymns were very full and express in proclaiming the *Divine nature* of Christ, and in offering him Divine worship—all which Paul abhorred.

3. In order to propagate his errors, this able and artful heretic felt it to be indispensable to abolish the use of these hymns.

4. In their place he enjoined the *exclusive use* of passages of Scripture, probably of the Psalms; at the same time denouncing the hymns as "modern compositions," and human inventions.

In conclusion, "we have all the evidence which specimens of undoubted antiquity can afford, that such scriptural hymns were early composed and used by Christians." Such is the testimony of the learned editors of the "Biblical Repertory" (for 1829), to which the reader is referred for many examples. The same authorities cite several most learned commentators to prove that Ephesians 5: 14—"Awake thou that sleepest," &c., 1 Timothy 3: 16, 2 Timothy 2: 11–13, are quotations from hymns in common use when the apostle wrote. The passage in Ephesians 5: 14 is expressly given by the apostle as a quotation, without any reference to its author or origin. Grotius and many others, regard the passage, Acts 4: 24–30, as a hymn, and Augustine calls it, "the first Christian Psalm." It was probably chanted after the manner of the Jews in their synagogues. "And Philo, a cotemporary of the Apostles, is reported by Nicephorus to have testified that the primitive Christians, after the time of Christ and the apostles, sang in their public worship not only the Psalms of David and other poems of Scripture, but also hymns or odes composed by themselves."* "It has been demonstrated," says the learned Bingham,† "that there were always such Psalms, and hymns, and doxologies composed by the pious (not inspired) men, and used in the church from *the first foundation* of it. Nor

* Biblical Repertory, 1829, pp. 526-539.

† Origines Ecclesiasticæ, vol. 4, p. 443.

did any but Paul of Samosata except against the use of them, which he did, because they contained a doctrine contrary to his own private opinions." Many of the extracts from early writers to prove these points, may be seen in the original languages, in Lord Chancellor King's "Enquiry into the Constitution and Worship of the Primitive Church," and still more fully in the great work of Bingham, quoted in the margin. Thus ecclesiastical history unites with the Holy Scriptures in condemning the *exclusive* system as an innovation upon apostolical institutions.

In view of the mass of evidence in these Letters, we cannot but indulge the hope that the needless and hurtful divisions and alienations originating in Psalmody, will soon cease. When that happy period shall arrive, these honored fathers and brethren whom we are now constrained to withstand, will be glad to copy the safe example of the ancient church of Scotland, and unite with her humble representative, the Presbyterian church—in their New Testament ascriptions of praise to the incomprehensible Jehovah, the Glorious Trinity in Unity—"the King eternal, immortal and invisible, the only wise God." Nor will it any longer be regarded as "a corruption of Divine worship," to say with Sternhold and Hopkins, and the early Scottish church:

To Father, Sonne, and Holy Ghost,
All glory be therefore;
As in beginning was, is now,
And shall be evermore:

And with Dr. Watts at the close of his hymns—"I cannot persuade myself to put a full period to these Divine hymns, till I have addressed a *special song* of glory to God the Father, the Son, and the Holy Spirit."

Thus did our Scottish forefathers delight to celebrate the praises of the adorable Trinity, which, as Dr. Watts expresses it, "is that *peculiar glory* of the Divine nature, that our Lord Jesus Christ has so clearly revealed to men, and *is so necessary* to true Christianity."

18

APPENDIX.

After most of the foregoing Treatise was written, there appeared in Philadelphia a volume entitled "The True Psalmody," which seems to demand a brief notice.

On the 16th of August, 1858, as we are told in the advertisement, a meeting was held in that city, which appointed Rev. J. M. Willson, J. T. Cooper and R. J. Black a committee "to prepare a work in favor of the exclusive use of the Scripture Psalmody." At a subsequent meeting, this committee reported such a treatise, and were unanimously authorized to publish it. Hence the volume called "True Psalmody," which professes to be "largely a compilation" from the treatises of Dr. M'Master, Pressly and others. Of course most of its arguments have been anticipated in the foregoing Letters. We add a few strictures.

1. The volume bears marks of *haste*. Thus, p. 117, we are told of "a touching hymn" with the title, "Veni *Sancta* Spiritus," "composed by King Robert of France, and in which all his gentle nature seems to speak." This professes to be a quotation from a volume called "The Voice of Christian Life." The committee should have corrected the *bad grammar*, either of King Robert or of the author of "The Voice." "*Sancta* Spiritus" is an unfortunate attempt at Latin.

Again: The running title of the work from p. 71 to p. 183, is "Hymns unwarranted." But here is a labored attempt to prove that when Paul speaks of "Psalms, *hymns* and spiritual songs," Ephesians 5 : 19, he intended by all these terms, only "David's Psalms." If this be so, then it follows that we have inspired authority to call "the Psalms" *hymns!* But the title of the book repeats more than a *hundred times*, "hymns unwarranted"—"hymns unwarranted," &c. It is only from other parts we learn that the committee mean "uninspired hymns," thus escaping the odium of having placed their ban upon David's *hymns,* as well as all the rest.

2. In their "Introduction" they say—"We believe most firmly * * * that this (the book of Psalms) should be in a *literal translation* sung in the worship of God." This is said while its authors use constantly "Rouse's paraphrase." Of course they do not sing a *translation* at all, but a patchwork paraphrase or "large *explication,*" as Ralph Erskine defines the term. This subject is fully discussed in our first six Letters, where will also be found a satisfactory answer to the committee's announcement—"we adhere to the *very matter* provided for us by Him whose praises we celebrate." These are very extraordinary statements, proceeding as they do from a learned committee. How strange that they should speak of Rouse as "the *very matter* provided by God!"

3. Following in the track of their predecessors, they set up "their man of straw" in various instances, and belabor it most lustily! For example, they charge those against whom they are arguing, with designing "to *supersede* the inspired and appointed manual," and to "introduce other Psalms or hymns" in its stead, pp. 46, 71. And their favorite epithets for those with whom they differ are, "the friends of human composition"—"advocates of human Psalmody"—just as though there were no human composition in Rouse! This volume, however, is rather more moderate in its phraseology than some we have noticed. Though it does not charge us in so many words, with "*impiously rejecting* the songs which God has given;" yet we are reminded of the danger of "offering strange fire!" The committee seem to have very complacently come to the conclusion, that their patchwork paraphrases are really "the songs composed in heaven." To attempt to disturb this pleasant dream would be only to repeat much that has been already said in our "Letters."

4. The materials which the committee have thrown

together in this "compilation," exhibit some curious examples of incoherence and discord. Nor is it easy to determine, of two or more conflicting sentiments set forth with equal zeal and authority, which they wish us to receive as their matured convictions. For example, in the "Introduction" they plead for — "The *book of Psalms* in a literal translation," "to the exclusion of uninspired songs," page 7. But when they reach page 217, their proposition is, "the *Psalms of Scripture* to the exclusion of all uninspired songs." But do the committee really believe that "the book of Psalms," and "the Psalms of Scripture," are identical in meaning? Are there no Psalms, hymns and spiritual songs in *Scripture*, except in the one book? Will they venture to maintain so absurd a proposition?

Again: On page 7 of the "Introduction," they plead for "the book of Psalms to the exclusion of all *uninspired* songs." But when they reach page 65, they quote a leading author as follows: "It would appear to be the Divine will that this (book of Psalms) should be used to *the exclusion of all others.*" This of course *excludes* not only "uninspired songs," but "all others" except the Psalms of David, both *inspired* and uninspired! Which side does the committee maintain, or wish us to adopt in this conflict of sentiment? And what is most extraordinary, on page 133, the committee themselves say—"The issue before us is, have we liberty to make and sing * * songs *other than those of the Bible!*" On page 7, it was "the book of Psalms to the exclusion of all uninspired songs," but when they arrive at page 133, they forsake their first position, "the book of Psalms," and are found arguing against "songs *other* than those of the Bible"—where of course they take under their protection not only "the book of Psalms," but "the songs of the Bible" generally, as well as those of the book of Psalms! The leading author whom they quote with so much approbation, says it appears to be "*the Divine will*" to exclude "all others" but "the Psalms;" but not so the committee when they arrive at page 133. They then say, it is "songs *other* than those of the Bible," against which they contend! At one time, it is "the book of Psalms" exclusively for which they are valiant — but at another "the songs of the Bible," including, of course, all *songs in the Bible*—in defense of which they have unsheathed the sword of controversy! And still more to confound this confusion, the committee tell us near the close of the book (p. 217), "We have kept but *one definite proposition* before us—*the Psalms of Scripture*, the church's sufficient and appointed manual of praise." So that this oracle of "True Psalmody" greatly needs an interpreter to expound its responses.

5. This "True Psalmody" is largely employed with objections to "uninspired hymns." "They have led," the committee tell us, "to the abandonment of congregational singing;" and "in domestic worship," they strongly intimate, "there is comparatively little use of sacred songs." These are unquestionably great evils; and so far as they exist among the advocates of hymns, deserve to be condemned. But have the committee traced these evils to the true cause, viz. the use of hymns? In a foot note they admit *a fact* which entirely spoils their argument. "The Methodist denominations" not only "retain congregational singing," as the committee concede—but as every one knows, make more use of *song* in Divine worship than all the other denominations put together! Yet these same Methodists do not sing "the Psalms" at all, but only hymns! The logic of "The True Psalmody" is sadly at fault here. Again, "the use of hymns endangers the church's purity: they have been used in diffusing error and heresy." But has not the pulpit been often used for the same purposes? Do not men *wrest* Scripture to their own destruction? Are the Scriptures and public preaching therefore to be discarded as dangerous to the purity of the church? Has not "the grace of God" often been abused to licentiousness? What, then, becomes of the committee's argu-

ment? Do not the Arians of Ulster sing and *explain* "Rouse's paraphrase" so as "to diffuse error and heresy?" Of course the use and explanation of "Rouse's paraphrase" should be abandoned as *endangering the purity of the church!*

6. From page 73 to page 96, we have a labored attempt from the pen of Dr. Cooper, to prove that Paul's "Psalms, hymns and spiritual songs" (Ephesians 5 : 19) must mean the Psalms of David exclusively. Dr. C. is no bad special pleader—but we merely refer him to the decision of Ralph Erskine, quoted in one of our Letters. He will there find the unbiassed judgment of a prince among the original fathers of Dr. C's. division of the United Presbyterian church, viz. that Ephesians 5 : 19, Colossians 3 : 16, contain "*a Divine precept*" for singing such human paraphrases as Erskine composed on "Solomon's Song." As Ralph Erskine had no peculiar dogma to defend, it is quite probable he was right, and Dr. C. altogether wrong.

In the same connection it is argued that "the sayings of Mary and the prophecy of Zacharias" (Luke 1) are no "precedents" in favor of New Testament songs—"for," they tell us, "of Mary it is merely stated that she '*said;*' her utterances are not styled *a song;* nor is there any evidence that she *sang* them."

Now as this argument has been employed in Pittsburgh, * as well as Philadelphia, it is worth a moment's attention. "Mary did not sing—she only *said.*" But in Revelation 5 : 9, we read—"they *sung* a new song, *saying*, Thou art worthy," &c. Hence it follows, that the four living creatures, and the four and twenty elders, did not *sing at all*—they only *said!* For other examples see Revelation 4 : 10, 5 : 12, 7 : 10–12. Try the same argument with some of the Psalms. "David *spake* unto the Lord the words of this *song.*" Psalm 18. Did David *say* or sing? Or is Psalm 18 a *song*? Again: "*I said,* I will take heed to my ways." Psalm 39. Of

* Pressly on Psalmody, p. 44.

course this Psalm is not to be sung, for David only "*said*" it! Again: Psalm 55—"*Sing* forth the honor of his name—make his *praise* glorious. *Say* unto God, how terrible art thou." The committee can perhaps decide whether this Psalm, like the 18th, is to be *said* or *sung*, since both terms are used!

Again: To account for the fact, asserted but not proved, "that singing praise has been *dropped* so extensively in connection with the use of hymns," the committee say "the *idea of worship has ceased* to no inconsiderable extent to be attached to the singing of hymns." To prove this extraordinary assertion, they quote "S. D." in the "Presbyterian," thus: "Protestants and Papists alike sing to creatures." "*We* sing to all sorts of inferior creatures, especially to sinners." But if this is sound argument, we wonder the committee have not long since "*dropped* the use of the Psalms!" Take this example from Psalm 52:

Why dost thou boast, O mighty man,
Of mischief and of ill.
Thy tongue mischievous calumnies
Deviseth subtilely.

If any *worse* example of "singing to creatures, especially to sinners," can be found in our hymns, we have never discovered it. Again, Psalm 94: 8—

Ye brutish people, understand!
Fools! when wise will ye grow?

For more of this dreadful *evil* of "singing to creatures and to sinners," see Psalms 49, 58, 62, 66, 67, 2, 4, 9, 10, and many others. If Dr. Cooper and his brethren will practice the doctrine they preach, and *drop* all such Psalms as these, we will begin to think they feel the force of their own argument. By their own showing, the Psalms of David "contribute influences to mislead the minds and corrupt the hearts of sinful men," equally in this particular with our hymns! When our Assembly shall issue an *expurgated* edition of our hymns, Dr. C. and his brethren of course will be found expurgating

David! Our system, they tell us, "needs amending and purging," p. 155. We reply, by your own showing, so does David!

On page 69, adopting the words of a leading author, the committee say—"One thing is certain, that neither our Lord nor his apostles have furnished any Psalms and songs for the use of the church." The committee surely do not think that saying "it is certain"—is the same as *proving* their proposition. But no man who carefully reads the New Testament, can for a moment doubt that there are *many* "songs" of praise in that volume; such for example, as those of Mary, and Simeon, and Zacharias, as well as those recorded in the Acts, the Epistles and the Revelation. Scores of passages can be readily adduced, having much more of the attributes of sacred "song," viz. sublime devotion and poetical excellence, than many of the more *prosaic* parts of the book of Psalms. This is so obvious, the wonder is that it has ever been called in question. All that is necessary is to have some poet, such as *Rouse* or *Watts*, to paraphrase these beautiful passages in verse and metre—and we have a volume of New Testament "songs." How strange that good men should venture to affirm that "our Lord and his apostles have furnished *no songs* for the church!" And this rash assertion includes "the new song," Rev. 5 : 9–14, recorded by the apostle John. It will not do to say "*it is certain* this 'new song' was not furnished *for the use* of the church." That is *the very point to be proved;* and which never was and never will be proved. The commentators teach a very different lesson.

To make this reasoning still more obvious, look at a few examples. Can any one doubt that there are many passages in the New Testament, at least, as worthy to be called "songs" and versified for purposes of praise as the following:

At evening they go to and fro:
They make great noise and sound,

Like to a dog, and often walk
About the city round.

And let them wander up and down
In seeking food to eat;
And let them grudge when they shall not
Be satisfied with meat.

Or these:

Whose belly with thy treasure hid
Thou fill'st—they children have
In plenty. Of their goods the rest,
They to their children leave.

When they me saw, they from me fled;
E'en so I am forgot
As men are out of mind when dead:
I'm like a broken pot.

These and scores of similar stanzas, are parts of songs of "*Divine institution*"—but the songs of the New Testament: "*None are furnished!*" But, say the committee, Prof. Alexander, of Princeton, affirms that all "the Psalms" are "songs, poems intended to be sung, and with a musical accompaniment;" and that "they are intended to *be permanently used* in the worship of God." But in what *manner* are they to be "permanently used?" What did Prof. A. mean by this language? "The learned and highly esteemed Professor" constantly uses our "Psalms and hymns," and in all probability never sung five stanzas of Rouse in his life! Yet the committee venture to quote him as favoring their notions of "a correct and *literal* translation!" The "permanent use" advocated by Prof. A. does not help the cause of "True Psalmody!" And then as to "the musical accompaniment," which the Professor says was also "intended"—the committee shrink from it with horror.

The committee endeavor to make a little capital out of the fact, that some hymns in frequent use were the productions of men who gave no evidence of being regenerated; and that Tom Moore's hymn beginning—"*Come ye disconsolate, where'er ye languish*"—is found in our collection. It can not be denied that our hymns in general are from Christian pens, from such eminent authors as Watts, Newton, Toplady, Cowper, Heber, Montgomery, &c. But one of these songs is the production of *Tom Moore*—that is "the dead fly in the ointment." Let us inquire whether nothing can be said in palliation of so great an enormity.

(1.) Do these brethren never *worship God* by reading or otherwise uttering the prayer of Baalam: "Let me die the death of the righteous, and let my last end be like his?" Numbers 23 : 10. Have they never worshiped God by reading from the pulpit his prophecies—"There shall come a star out of Jacob, and a sceptre shall rise out of Israel," &c.? Are these prophecies and this prayer *the worse*, because their author was not a regenerate man?

(2.) Is not a large part of the book of Job the utterance of error? Does not the Lord tell Eliphaz —"My wrath is kindled against thee and against thy two friends; for ye have not spoken of me the thing *which is right?*" Chapter 42 : 7. But do not these brethren worship God by reading publicly these false sentiments?

(3.) When "the devils," in various instances, acknowledged Jesus to be the true Messiah, "the Holy One of God," he did not command them to be silent—he did not refuse a recognition of his Divine character and mission even from "devils." Yet our brethren *worship God* by reading from their pulpits these just and true ascriptions of honor to Christ, though their authors were *the devils!* Is not this almost as bad as singing a hymn of Tom Moore? If the committee feel no "compunctious visitings" while worshiping God in the language of "Balaam the son of Bosor, who loved the wages of unrighteousness," (2 Peter 2 : 15,) with the false sentiments of Job's friends, against whom God's "wrath was kindled"—and even in the language of "the devils" of the New Testament—then what becomes of their argument? Doubtless even wicked men are sometimes deeply impressed with Divine things, as Balaam was, and are so under the teaching of the Holy Spirit as to utter many most valuable and interesting truths. And if, after the manner of Balaam, they possess the most elevated poetic talents — we think the scriptural examples do not condemn the occasional use of their utterances in public worship. Certainly the committee are not in a position "to cast the first stone" at us Presbyterians.

6. The "True Psalmody" has much to say against "uninspired songs," "human composition," &c. And the committee say they "are certainly at liberty to pronounce *very decidedly* the Scottish version ("Rouse's paraphrase") to be an *accurate rendering* of the original." Not to repeat what has already been said in our Letters, take these specimens from Psalm 102 : 6—

> Like pelican in wilderness
> Forsaken I have been.
> I like an owl in desert am
> That nightly there doth moan.

Will these brethren inform us where they find in "the original," the second and fourth of these lines? And the same is true of hundreds of similar stanzas. They are specimens of *Rouse's composition*. Yet Dr. P. speaks of Rouse as "the *Divine songs* in this version," including, of course, all the sentiment and verbiage which he has added to the inspired text! The committee must not be surprised to hear from every intelligent Presbyterian, in reply to such argument — "Physician, heal thyself." And are they certain Rouse was "a regenerate person?" If not — "how dare they sing his effusions?"

7. The closing chapter of "The True Psalmody" is employed in lauding "the version," i. e. Rouse's poetry. But in addition to the testimony of Dr. Cooper and others adduced in our Letters, we have room only for the following: At the General Assembly of the United Presbyterian church at Xenia, in May, 1859, a resolution was adopted, "that the version of the book of Psalms (Rouse) now used by the United Presbyterian church, be retained, without any change that would affect its integ-

rity." In the debate on this resolution, as reported in "The Preacher," the Rev. Mr. Van Eaton said—"He could not be brought to express any admiration for its blemishes, its positive *ugliness*. * * * The version was not argued against — it *was simply laughed at*. Those who had not been educated to it from childhood, *could not use it at all*. It had been said that other versions, and collections of hymns, were *sectarian*. The Psalms were catholic, but *the version was sectarian*. It was just as certain as doom, that if the United Presbyterian church were bound down to the old version, she becomes exclusively an old country church, Scotch-Irish, and nothing more. The Psalms were God's Psalms—were inspired—but the version was not inspired. He hoped the church would not clog herself with this old and imperfect version." Comment is needless.

We here dismiss "The True Psalmody." We have endeavored to give the work that "careful investigation," that "devout and prayerful examination," which the committee recommend to "the candid inquirer after truth and duty." p. 11. If the result has not been such as they seem to have anticipated, it is no fault of ours.

NOTE.

Dr. James Latta.—"The True Psalmody," p. 162, exhibits Dr. L., whose "Discourse on Psalmody" is out of print, as "in the service of the infidel," viz. by "representing *the Psalms* of the Bible as unchristian in spirit, in doctrine—unfit for devotion, tending to make heretics," &c. Very different is the judgment of the late venerable and excellent Dr. Miller, Professor in the Theological Seminary at Princeton. He says—"Dr. Latta, for talents and learning, as *well as piety*, held a *high place* among the clergy of his day. He published a 'Discourse on Psalmody,' which '*does honor to his memory*.'" *Memoir of Dr. Rodgers*, p. 178. Every reader can decide which of these witnesses is the more likely to be true. Dr. Miller certainly never could have apologized for any "utterances against the word of God," either by Dr. Latta, or any other author.

www.ingramcontent.com/pod-product-compliance
Lightning Source LLC
LaVergne TN
LVHW011207110826
845150LV00006B/1346

* 9 7 8 1 4 2 5 5 1 8 2 9 5 *